Hat Talk

Conversations with Hat
Makers about Their Hats—
the Fedora, Homburg,
Straw, and Cap

by Debbie Henderson, Ph.D.

The Wild Goose Press

This project was funded by the Traveling Hat Salesmen's Association of America.

Published by the Wild Goose Press, 504 Phillips Street, Yellow Springs, OH 45387

ISBN 0-9651153-6-4

Photo Credits
I am grateful to the following for permission to reprint the photographs that appear on these pages:
Danbury Museum and Historical Society, viii, 3, 8, 9, 15
John Brandwood, 24
Robert Doran, 33, 34, 37
Graham Thompson, 128

© 2002 Debbie Henderson

Printed in Korea by Graphics International

Book design by Jane Baker

Contents

Introduction　　　　　　　　　　　　　　　　v

1 Danbury, Connecticutt:
   The Town That Crowns Them All　　　　1

2 Gentlemen's Hatters and Their Hats:
   Knox, Dunlap, Cavenaugh, Dobbs, Bollman,
   Langenberg, and Borsalino　　　　　　17
   Conversation with Robert Doran　　　　*31*

3 The System of Hat Making:
   Stetson, Resistol, Steven's Hat Companies　43
   Conversations with Hat Company
   Executives　　　　　　　　　　　　　*45*

4 Everyman and His Bowler　　　　　　65

5 How the Fedora Got Its "Snap"　　　　75
   Conversations with Hat Salesmen　　　*84*

6 The Disposable Straw　　　　　　　　95
   Conversation with John Milano　　　　*103*

7 A Chap and His Cap　　　　　　　　113

8 The Trouble with Hats　　　　　　　　119

   Appendix　　　　　　　　　　　　　129
   John B. Stetson Catalogues
   for 1913, 1914, and 1915　　　　　　134

   Notes　　　　　　　　　　　　　　　143

   Bibliography　　　　　　　　　　　　149

This book would not have been possible were it not
for the many hat makers, hat salesmen, and hat
wearers who gave of their valuable time in the telling
of their stories.

In addition, there would be no book or hat collection
without the support and enthusiasm of my husband,
Jon Barlow Hudson. It is to him that this book is
dedicated, with love and appreciation.

Many thanks to Richard Spencer
for his continued editorial help.

Jon Barlow Hudson, sculptor

Introduction

"We can distinguish by the taste of the hat, the mode of the wearer's mind."
—George "Beau" Brummell, *Male and Female Costume*

When is it that a person realizes that the world around her has changed? When I was a child, I saw my father wearing a suit, topcoat, and fedora to work. I watched TV and movies with men wearing hats.

I was an impressionable teen when we dressed in what now looks like "mommy" clothes—dress, stockings, coat, hat, and gloves for church (garter belts and bras included).

I was a college student when the sixties hit full blast. I tossed my bra, stockings, and garter belt, along with church hats and matching suits. Hats were no longer required; they became a symbolic accessory. Why, then, the fascination with hats? Why worry about a fashion piece that has had its day? Men in the hatting industry don't feel that the man's hat has seen its end, its finish, even though the number of hat-producing factories has dwindled from over one hundred in 1900 to under ten in 2000. It wasn't just John F. Kennedy not wearing a top hat in 1960 that caused the change. Hat-wearing had slowly been declining since the automobile became popular. Hats were no longer needed for protection and, in some sportier cars, were impossible to wear.

That's when I realized that pieces of clothing mean much more than their cut, style, or fiber content. The times, the personality of the wearer, the crowd, the culture—all influence, and are influenced by, clothing. Look at family photographs and you can start sensing the personality of an era, and the personality of your relatives.

We know hats were worn by men since the beginning of pictorial history— crowned pharaohs in Egypt, helmeted crusaders, turban-covered sheiks—and gave panache to dandified gentlemen in tall top hats, who tipped them politely or rudely according to custom and desire. Hats are the final statement to an ensemble—the punctuation. I still wear a hat when I want to be noticed. When my husband wears any of his ten-gallon western hats or pastel Borsalino fedoras, he is looked at, commented on, and (as I observe) admired.

Maybe that is why I love hats.

What I learned from research was far broader. The hat has not only a fashion history, but also an anthropological social history, a manufacturing history, and an economic history as well, as does all clothing.

In *Cowboys and Hatters: Bond Street, Sagebrush and the Silver Screen* I gave an overview of the hatting history. *The Top Hat* focused on a particular type of hat, while in *The Handmade Felt Hat*, I explored a process. In this book I am looking at a century, more specifically the changes that occurred between the hat-wearing beginning of the twentieth century, and the hat as one element of eclectic dress in the second half of the century.

I have found many ways to tell this story, most importantly through interviews with the people who created this history as manufacturers and sellers of hats. There is a review of some of the more famous brands of hats, such as Borsalino, Stetson, Resistol, Bollman, Biltmore, Knox, and Dunlap, as well as a sketch of that famous hat-making town, Danbury, Connecticut. What these people and their companies manufactured, and how their hats were worn, is illustrated in photographs of men wearing hats. Other rare sources are the company hat catalogues. When I first started this research I thought sales catalogues would be abundant and the easy way to identify and date men's hats. Sadly, the majority have been lost or destroyed, which is why I have included pages from the few catalogues that I have discovered. If you happen to stumble across some in your attic, hold on to them!

I encourage you to use this as a beginning to your own research. Think of starting your own album. Ask your relatives about their hat-wearing (or any type of clothing you prefer). Collect their stories and pictures. It never fails; everyone has a hat story (usually many).

The man's hat is a survivor. The Borsalino sales representative said that hats in a pastel color range were "in." Stetson and Resistol reps say that the western style hat is strong in the West, while straw fedoras with wider brims protect faces and necks in sunnier climates. The baseball cap is everywhere as part of the contemporary fashion picture. Each year the industry shifts. One hat salesman said that at a 1950 sales convention only about two hours were spent talking about the western hat; now the "cowboy" style supports much of the straw and fur felt business.

This book is a tribute to the people responsible for making, selling, and wearing hats. Thank them for their devotion to the production of "a quality product"—go out and buy a hat!

Debbie Henderson, Ph.D.
Yellow Springs, Ohio
March, 2002

Hat Talk

*George Schweitzer, superintendent at Frank H. Lee Company, inspecting fur felt cones for flaws and "dags."
Courtesy of the Danbury Museum & Historical Society.*

1

Danbury, Connecticut: The Town That Crowns Them All

> "Hatting has been the means of building up our Village, filling it with an industrious population, and infusing into it all the bustle of trade and ceaseless activity. It is the life of the place, the mainspring to all success and advancement."
> —William H. Francis, 1856

Danbury's connection with hatting started before the American Revolution. Because earlier records were destroyed when the British burned the town, the first hatter on record is Zadoc Benedict, listed in 1780 with two apprentices in a hat business on Main Street. In those days a hatter might also be a farmer, making hats for local customers during the quiet winter months, so most probably there were other hatters crafting fur felt hats in their homes.

Danbury was a good place to produce hats. It had the necessary requirements: access to fur, plenty of water in the Still River, fuel to heat the water, manpower, and relatively easy access to broader markets, New York City in particular. More small shops popped up. Oliver Burr brought men from England. By 1787 the partnership of Burr and White kept thirty journeymen and apprentices busy. So rapid was the growth that by 1801, the Reverend Thomas Robbins bragged in his Century Sermon, "In the manufacture of hats, this town much exceeds any one in the United States. More than 20,000 hats, mostly of fur, are made annually for exportation."[1]

For a litttle over a century, the hatting industry in Danbury drove the town's economy. William H. Francis, who compiled a history of hatters in 1856, wrote that by that year (nine years before John B. Stetson founded his brand), Danbury was sending hats all across the continent. Production of one and a half million hats in 1859 rose to four and a half million in 1880 and to five million in 1887.[2] During a convention of hat manufacturers in 1885, thirty-one of the sixty-three manufacturers present were from Danbury. Danbury firms supplied

Hawes, von Gal advertisement in the American Magazine in the early 1900s.

specific chains, for example the von Gal Company, which exclusively supplied the Hawes chain of stores. The Frank H. Lee Company, founded in 1909, sold more hats than any other company in America, supplying J. C. Penny until production and sales stopped three-quarters of the way through the twentieth century. It was a boom town for hats.

Fortunately for history, men who worked, and who still work, in the hat industry are willing to tell its story. George Rafferty is one. George, who started in the hatting business as a youngster, was one of the last to manage the big shops before they shut down. His words make vivid a Danbury thriving during the boom period of hat making; we can only mourn its demise.

Of the many big-name brands started in Danbury, some are still familiar today. Others are forgotten. Among these, Tweedy, White, and Company, labeled "the most extensive furriers since the time of Astor," were in the fur-cutting business, processing approximately 100,000 pelts annually.[3] The Taylor family in 1822 invented the dye wheel for coloring multiple hat bodies, which saved time and labor. James S. Taylor invented a sizing machine that dominated the industry for seventy years.[4] Charles Reed devised a brim-rounding machine. Two nephews, John C. and James F. Doran, founded Doran Brothers, a company that invented and sold finishing machines all over the world.[5] Machines increased production while the railroad spread that production across the country.

Brand names still recognizable today include Lee, Disney (a Lee line), Adam, and Mallory. In 1909 Frank H. Lee, son of Irish immigrants, built a large plant in Danbury. Lee's hats were in direct competition with Mallory and Stetson. Ezra Mallory, a farmer, started making hats in 1823. By 1856 E. A. Mallory Company had ninety-five employees, a capital of $20,000, and manufactured 8,640 dozen hats a year for a sales total of $155,000. Sons Charles and William joined their father, as did a great-grandson, Harry B. Mallory. The company thrived in Danbury until it was sold in the 1960s. George Rafferty managed production for both of these hatting giants.

But hatlessness was in the wind. Some say it started after World War II, but Bob Doran of Doran Bros. says the decline of the man's hat started much earlier. Knowing that he would go into the family business, even in college Bob Doran paid attention to clothing trends. His study of outerwear sales figures, done in 1941 at Notre Dame, indicated that sales, not only of men's hats, but of all items of men's outerwear, were decreasing.

> I wrote to the Department of Commerce and I got production figures of what I informally classified as men's weather apparel. I started with felt hats, galoshes,

1. Danbury, Connecticut

Frank H. Lee Company, ca. 1920. Courtesy of the Danbury Museum and Historical Society.

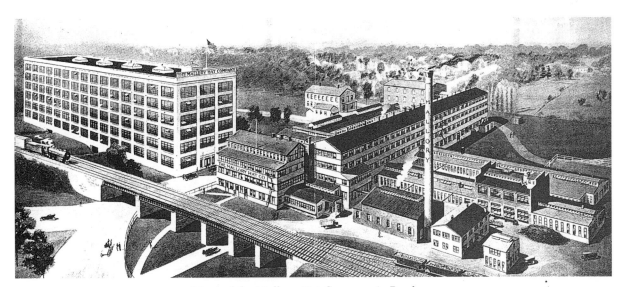

Plant of the Mallory Hat Company in Danbury.

woolen scarves, non-work mittens and gloves, heavy overcoats, woolen underwear—everything I could quickly classify as weather apparel for men. I took 1920 as a base figure and for the same period I got the production figures for the automotive industry. I graphed them out. The men's apparel lines started to decline in parallel lines to the inverse curve to the automotive curve. You didn't need that kind of clothing anymore. You had your peak from the development of the form-ing machine up until about the turn of the century. This was in the United States and Europe. In the U.S. in 1903 the men's hat industry made three and a half million to four million dozen men's hats with a population of about eighty million people. They had about 350 formers operating in the U.S. in 1900. This was a real gradual thing and most hatters never saw it and didn't recognize it.[6]

The protective automobile and central heating, as well as the relief of former soldiers at not having to wear

"Your hat is not just one of a collection of things to wear, like your shirt or cravat. It is completely isolated from the rest of your dress by your face. Of all articles that a man assumes his hat alone fully, freely and flexibly interprets his personality. Your suit is buttoned on; your collar is fastened on; your scarf is tied on; your hosiery is drawn on; your glove is squeezed on; your shoe is laced on, but your hat alone is *put* on.

"Your hat, by its quality and individuality; poise and pitch; angle and droop can be made to take on as many varying moods as the face underneath. A hat may look aristocratic or vulgar; serious or humorous; gloomy or cheerful; dignified or flippant; radical or conservative; rakish or righteous; fresh or wilted; alive or dead.

"Your hat is YOU. It commends or condemns you. It bestows character or becomes a caricature. Hence, it should not be selected at random, but chosen with care, to be a reflection of the wearer's taste, position and personality, instead of a reflection upon them. Moreover, your hat, being on the direct level of the observer's line of vision, is the first thing his eye sees and judges. Thus, a really fine hat is not just a disbursement to cover the head, but an investment in individuality, self-respect and the respect of others."

From Beaver's Back, to Man's Head, C. A. Mallory, President, The Mallory Hat Company

hats, made the difference. A few short fashion spurts helped stave off disaster. The "Empress Eugenie" women's hat craze,[7] movies such as *Raiders of the Lost Ark*, *Urban Cowboy,* and western mania have kept the hat business going.[8]

Many of the Danbury companies saw what was coming. As Bob Doran explained, he knew that sales were declining as men decided to wear hats less frequently. Some firms diversified. Doran Bros. made machines for the dairy industry, but even they eventually sold out, closing their doors on two centuries of

1. Danbury, Connecticut

Danbury's history.

Conversation with George Rafferty

March 9, 1999

DH: When did you get started?

GR: I went to work at Mallory's in 1929, right in the middle of the depression. You know, the hatters were not hurt as badly as the rest of the country. One thing that nobody talks about is women's hats. In those days women's hats were a big item. They kept us going in the off seasons. Generally women had just three colors—black, brown, and navy. We would stock those colors in the off season. Hatting was very seasonable. You were always working a season ahead. You had to hold all that stock until you shipped it. The ladies' hats used to carry us quite a bit. We made a lot of them. I remember when the Empress Eugenie hat was big—a very simple hat—we couldn't make enough of them. The trucks would come up from New York. There were never any ladies' hats finished in Danbury. Lee and John Green were the only ones who had finishing factories. Ladies' hats, never. Maybe a girl in town finished a few. All of them were out of town. When that Princess Eugenie rush was on, those trucks would come up in the afternoon, and they'd wait for the day's production. When that last hat was out of the door, the truck would go to New York. That went on for a couple of months. We made so many ladies' hats.

I went to work young. Of course, in those days, you just went to work. I was the youngest of ten. My mother and father had raised us all, and I was the last one home. My mother and father built the first home they ever had. My father worked on the railroad. We were struggling along. One day I went down to Mallory and I got a job. I worked there for two weeks before my parents found out. Of course, in those days, they used to have a truant officer who came around. He came around when I went home that night. Boy, did I get hell! They didn't want it. But every bit helps.

Look, between you and me, I didn't have no feeling to go farther in school. I said I'd go back to school, but I never did. It was just as well for me. Some of the guys that went to school were working for me later on. I was just fortunate that there was hatting in Danbury, and I happened to work my way up. I had a good life in hatting. I don't resent one day. I used to like it. When the boss would say, "Will you work here?" I always did. And I'm glad I did. I learned more that way. Other kids would say no. So I had the opportunity to work on most everything. I made good money, too. I'd have made more money had I gone to school—maybe, maybe not. Hat-

George Rafferty (right) with Jon Barlow Hudson

"*I had a good life in hatting. I don't resent one day.*"

ters worked hard, but they made good money.

In Danbury you either worked in the hat shop or the machine shop, because they built the hat machinery there, too. In Danbury there was never a section that was for poor people; Danbury never had a slum because hatters all had their own homes.

In those days in Danbury there were, basically, the Irish, the Polish, the Italians—three of them. When they came over, they went to the section of the town where the Polish and where the Irish people were. They lived in their own section. Not that they were mad at someone, but they felt more at home. You naturally would if you came from Europe. They all worked together in the factory. Some of the things they'd call each other! But it was all in fun. They'd go out at night and have a beer together. There was an old saying in Danbury, "There's more hats made in the taverns than there are in the factory."

Of course, with Lee and Mallory there was great competition. Mallory always said, "You guys don't know how to make hats." They [Lee] were making the low-end hats, but they were just as good hatters making those cheap hats, because you had to be a little more clever. We all had a good life together.

I liked the men. I liked the women. They were all good people.

DH: Were there many women working there?
GR: Oh yes, in the trimming room. It was mostly all women. We had our little squabbles now and then, like you will; but basically, you couldn't work with finer people. Of course, we had bad days like anybody. All in all, I had a good rapport with all of the people.

Mallory was union. I had one fellow was a steward in the shop. Sometimes they'd cause problems. The guys weren't complaining; we used to squabble a lot—nothing real. We'd squabble, he'd call me this, he'd call me that, but actually we were close. When Virginia and I celebrated our fiftieth wedding anniversary, we got this card. It says, "I suppose you'll be as surprised getting this as I am sending it!" and it was from him. He wasn't all that bad.

DH: Did you make military hats?

GR: In Canada at Biltmore they made the Royal Canadian hats and army hats. They're a pain in the neck because of inspections. The inspector would come around and the color had to be perfect. That was mostly wartime that we were doing that. I did get a call later from one of them in Philadelphia. He said we got a bid and we didn't hear from you. And I said, "No." He said, "You got to." And I said," You're not going to either!" I said, "When the war starts and they start shooting the guns, and they tell me I've got to make them—in the meantime, NO!"

DH: It's not so much the hat, but the government regulations?

GR: Yes, the regulations. They weren't worth it. We spent a lot more time making them.

DH: Did you make Boy Scout hats?

GR: No, never made any Boy Scout hats. Trooper hats were for Connecticut and also Missouri. They were good business. We used to make some for New Jersey. We didn't actually finish the hats. There was a fellow who had a little shop in New Jersey and he finished them up. He died, but I think his son is still running it, in Newark. Al Boum—his name was Al L. Boum. Stewart is the son.

DH: How did Stetson get started making trooper hats?

GR: I don't know how he got started. Steven, the father, was the old man. We made bodies for him. He eventually got tied in with Hat Corp in Winchester—used to get bodies from Winchester.

DH: That's a good place. They make good bodies.

GR: Yes.

DH: They've bought quite a lot of machinery from France. I guess that's about the only place you can find it.

GH: Yes. Yes. We got the machinery up in Danbury from this company in South Hatfield that went out of business. It was made in Italy. It was nice machinery. Some of the formers we set up. They had a fellow that would come up and help us set it up. That was in the agreement. I said to him, "We don't have that money for development. How come you can do it?" He said, "You paid for it, right after World War II. We had to spend it on something, so—"

DH: Is there any machinery left in Danbury or is it all gone?

GR: No, it's all gone. There's none in Danbury now. Whoever took it, Hat Brands or whoever, they must have taken it all down to Texas with them. No, but we made the machinery in Danbury when hatting was going good.

DH: Doran Bros.?

GR: Doran made mostly front shop machinery and Turner made the cones.[11] Then Genest, they invented the Genest machine. They were made in Danbury. They mechanized a lot of the hat making. In the old days it was all hand work. The machines made good hats too. When I was a kid, the sizing machines were—when the hats get down to a certain size, then they have to be final sized. Those are the ones, the final size—they came out of the color room. The dye bath, they'd save one barrel and they'd put the lot number on it, so when the lot came through the sizer, they would have that dye to keep it from bleeding. When I was a kid we used to have to go down into the color room. We had a big vat. They'd give us a number, and we'd have to run down, and we'd get seven pails, and we'd put them in this thing. At night we'd look like Indians—splatter all over.

DH: What was the dye made of? Did it wash off?

GR: Oh yes, it would wash off. You have all different dyes and you mix them. You have the dye machines. You have to put them in together. We had big drums. They'd hold fifty dozen of the small hats, twenty-five dozen of the big hats, and we would have to put them in the water with acid, and they would tumble at night, not tumble completely. You'd have to get the body to acidify or it wouldn't take the dye. And then in the morning, you would put the dye in and watch it as it went along, bring it up and boil it. Every once in a while you would check it, take it out, and then you'd put the sulfuric acid

*"Ragging" process. Man in foreground may be Nelson Ganley of Bethel.
Courtesy of Danbury Museum & Historical Society.*

on it, because otherwise, it [the color] would run.
DH: Then you would have to wash that off?
GR: Yeah, so there was a lot to it—more than people think.
DH: Very complex.
GR: Then the brims all had to be stiffened with shellac. We used to get the shellac from over in India. They used to send it flaked. Then we'd have to cook it. The water on that had to be on the acid side too. You cook it and you have to cook it so long. When it was set, then you'd put that on the brims. The western hats took a lot of stiffening.
DH: How is it that earlier hats could be made with a fine thin felt? Western hats today are thick felt.
GR: It all depends how you make it. I got a couple here [*shows hats*].

[In showing a list of hat manufacturers, George points out that not all the companies were big; some only had two formers.]

Here is the Stetson factory; it was a monster. Here is Mallory's [factory]—it was perfect [*shows floor plan*]. Here is the back shop where the fur came in and the hat bodies were made. There was a tunnel under the road here that went over. This was a six-story building, and there was an elevator that took the hat bodies up to the top floor. As each operation was done, it went down. By the time it got down to the bottom, it was done. They had it right under their hands, and they let it go. Instead of this big monster, running here, running there. This guy don't know what the hell that guy's doing. Mallory had the perfect setup for them. And they weren't smart enough to do it.

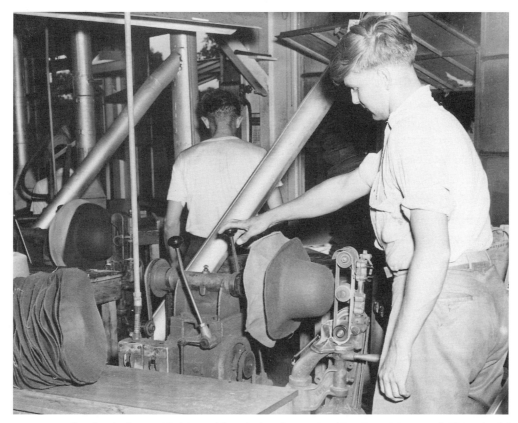

"Crown pouncer" in back shop at H. McLachlan & Co. Courtesy of Danbury Museum & Historical Society.

This is about Knox and Dobbs [*shows pamphlet*]. Knox and Dobbs were originally in Brooklyn. Later on, they moved to East Norwalk, Connecticut. Knox, Dobbs, and Cavenaugh—they were the high class. Cavanaugh was the top of the line. They had two plants in East Norwalk. They were Hat Corp. of America at that time. They made a lot of hats—good ones. I worked there for a while when it was slow up here. They needed somebody. I used to drive back and forth from here.

Mallory, I think, has one of the oldest hat labels in the United States, of anyone. I think 1923—before then even, 1819—

Here's Lee [*shows pamphlet*]. They produced more hats than anybody. They were in the middle range. They had a monstrous plant down there. Lee used to make a lot of hats for J. C. Penny. You see, Penny's at that time was not as high class as they are today. They used to buy what we'd call a 4-line. It had a little edge, a band something like on that western hat there, and a regular weight hat, not real light. It was a farmer's hat. We had a warehouse down in Lee's, and they'd give us an order, and we'd ship them out all over the country. We did big business.

You know, Stetson had the world by the tail and they let it go. They had a tremendous plant in Philadelphia when John B. founded it, but when it gets to the children it gets lost. Stetson was big because of their western hats. There were a lot of other hatters too. They were—I don't like to say snobbish, but Stetson had the name. The problem they got into, in my opinion—I was superintendent of Mallory's at the time when they bought Mallory's. What they were doing was trying to get enough business to keep that big monster going. I worked for them for about six months. Frank H. Lee Company was the biggest, the most productive. They were like the Ford and the Chevy. They produced more hats than anybody.

The father [Lee] had died and he had three sons and a daughter. They weren't what the old man was, but the daughter should have been running the company. She married an accountant in town. She went to court and she had trustees appointed and one of them was the mayor, one was head of the hospital, and one head of the utilities. That's how I got to Lee's. I knew the mayor for years. He called me and asked if I could come down and see him, down at Lee's. He said, "They've got this factory and they don't know anything about running it, and I don't know what we're going to do." I knew that Stetson would eventually close Mallory, so I'd go to Lee's as superintendent down there. Al Stever became the superintendent over at Mallory and we had a plan to consolidate everything up here. Mallory had everything, and Mallory could have taken care of the business of all of them. Eventually they [Stetson] bought off all of them. Eventually they [Stetson] bought Lee's too. I thought, "How long is this going to last?"

Then the Steven's Hat Company got involved. There was Ben Rosenthal, Gary Rosenthal's father and he was the finest guy. (Gary was a chip off the old block.) He heard that Stetson had bought Lee and he called me because I used to take care of him personally. I used to finish some hats for him. He had a little shop, but nothing like we had out here. So we got quite close. He heard Stetson had bought Lee. He sent me two airline tickets, so we went out there [St. Joseph, MO]. He said, "It's not going to last long there." In the meantime, he had bought a little three-former shop in Bethel [CT] and he didn't know how to run it. They had a finishing shop. The back shop and the finishing shop are two different things. He said, "I got a three-former shop now, do you want to come to work for me?" Ben and I got along well. That was about 1964. He never bothered me be-

cause he was glad to get somebody to run it. We used to make up bodies for a lot of different jobbers around New York. We made up some western hats for down in Texas. Like renovation stores, and they'd make up their own hats. Some of them had pretty good business down there.

DH: Was the company called Steven's Hat Company then?

GR: Yes, Steven's Hat Company. We were going along pretty good then. We only had three formers. We had a call one day from Cranston Braler (you never met him). He was a big wheel in Stetson. I had worked for him up here in Danbury; he was the boss over everything. He said, "Could you make a few bodies?" So I figured he had a friend or somebody who had a little shop, and they needed a few bodies. I said, "Sure, how many do

1. Danbury, Connecticut

you want?" "5,000 dozen," he said. I said, "5,000 dozen!" He said, "We're having a little problem, got in a backlog here. Could you make 5,000 dozen?" I said, "Sure," because there were a lot of hatters around at that time in Danbury, and so we put on a night shift right away. And we kept working and we didn't give up any of our other customers, and we finally got 5,000 dozen. I called him. He said, "Make 5,000 more." "What's wrong down there?" He says, "Well, we're having trouble." We started on the other 5,000. He called in the meantime about something special. Meanwhile, this Mallory backshop is lying idle across town, and I said to him, more of a joke, why don't you let us have that big plant over there, and then you'd have no more trouble. He said, "Ah, yeah." Eventually that came to be.

And Stevens—we went up there to open that plant up. They were to be 50-50. Stevens owned 50 percent, Stetson owned 50 percent. We went up there. Of course, the plant had been shut down for a year or two—everything had been shut down for a year or two. Everything had to be put in order. My son was an electrician and he had a contractor's license, so I said to him, "Give me a couple of guys to check the shop." They did and got it all fixed up. We opened up February 4, 1968.

Ben called me one night. He said, "I got a call from Dave Harshaw, the president of Stetson. He's a nice man, but no hatter. I don't care what business you're running, you never depend on anyone else, you should know what it is yourself, because they can tell you all kinds of stories. They shipped their backshop down to Philadelphia. We made all of their [Stetson's] bodies. We started in February 1968. We had hatters who could run all of the machinery, so when we started, to the end of that year, we made 74,000 dozen bodies.

DH: That's a lot of hats.

GH: Well, when you have thirteen formers— [A former is expected to turn out about forty dozen hat bodies a day; because Westerns are bigger, about thirty are the daily quota.]

So we got them. We're sending them bodies. They're finishing them. There was another man who got into the Stetsons. He bought into it, more or less, as a write-off, Ira Guilden. He saw how the back shop was running, and he said, "What the hell, why are we running this plant in Philadelphia?" So he got ahold of Ben [Rosenthal]. He said, "How about finishing our hats? They put up a building out in St. Joe. Eventually they shut down the Philadelphia plant completely. We would make the bodies to send them out to St. Joe and they would finish them. It was a good set-up because we had a fur shop in Newark. All your fur comes into the port. We didn't have to ship it around the Horn. We'd pick it up and send it up to Danbury.

DH: Saratelli Fur Company?

GR: Oh yes. We sent the bodies out in bundles. Of

course, St. Joe was in the middle of western business. You know what it would cost to send a container of finished hats? This way the bodies went out. The shipping to Texas and Wyoming from St. Joe wasn't so bad, so that went great. We did really well. Then Ben died. This Ira Guilden had a daughter and I guess she wanted to get into the hat business and then they wanted to buy it back [their 50 percent from Stevens Co.] So they made an offer. There were two brothers and they wanted the money, so they decided to sell. But now it belongs to HatCo. You know, they're not the same. It's a shame. It's a mismatch. They got Resistol, Dobbs, and Knox. You should make one, like Chevrolet. I don't know how they're doing. I talk to Gary once in a while. I never ask how they're doing. I retired because I figured I wouldn't be there long anyway.

DH: When did you retire?

GR: About ten years ago—just when this deal went through.

DH: Were there other places in the United States producing hats? It sounds like Danbury was producing all the hats. Langenberg was producing then.

GR: There was Stetson in Philadelphia. There was McLachlan, George and Harry McLachlan, but they didn't finish hats. They only did bodies, only a back shop. One was on Main Street, one was on a side street. Down in Orange, New Jersey, they had some.

DH: But not many places. Danbury was the center?

GR: Oh, Danbury made—this was before the decline—all the shops combined made 440,000 dozen hats in a year.

In the 30s and 40s there was a lot of production. All the factories were running—often ran two shifts.

Lee used to have Walter Winchel, the top commentator in those days, fifteen minutes every night. Lee sponsored him. Then Madison Square Garden used to have fights every Friday night—not televised, on the radio. Adam Hats, they sponsored them, too.

When they [the factories] were busy, you could drive around at night and you could hear the formers.

DH: Is Saratelli the only fur supplier?

GR: Oh no. We had our own sources. The man that ran the fur company used to buy it. That was down in Newark. His name was Norman Karp.

DH: Is his company still in business?

GR: I don't know, the way things have changed.

DH: Where did the majority of the fur come from?

GR: France. Years back it used to come from Australia, that was the best because it was all wild. They ran wild. But then they got so wild that the government started to cut back on it, so they're from France. The French, I guess, eat a lot of rabbit stew. They grow them on farms over there. But the wild ones were always the best. On the farms they wanted to fatten them, so they fed them. What they used to feed them used to give us a problem. The fur would be greasy. And when it was greasy, when you would try to form it (you saw the cone), it wouldn't

big screen. On a rabbit it's not all fur. There's hair too, and the hair didn't have any of those little barbs to felt. The fur has little barbs. The hair is dropped. The more you blew it, the finer the fur. On cheap hats you'd probably use an eight-section blower, and then on your better hats you'd use a twelve. A beaver has no barbs at all on it. They say 100 percent beaver. You can't make 100 percent beaver. You have to use some other—we used to use hares' fur. Because hares' fur is the next best thing, the strongest. We used to mix hares' fur with beaver so it was solid.

DH: Was chinchilla ever used?

GR: I don't know. It was a big difference when we stopped getting wild fur. Anything that's out in the wild is better. That's why the beaver skins we used to get from Canada, the winter skins, were so good.

DH: What about nutria? Is there enough?

GR: No, hard enough time getting enough rabbits. Of course, they're not making so many hats. If they were making the amount they used to—

The hats used to go out open-crowned and then Lee got into preshaping. They were the first ones that did it. Then everyone got into copying it, but Lee was the first one to make the preshaped hat.

DH: Were they still using wooden blocks?

GR: Oh yes, they still use wooden blocks.

DH: They weren't using aluminum blocks?

GR: The biggest use of aluminum was in pre-shaping in the front shop and some in the back shop hand blocking, but not much. They used to use aluminum blocks in the back shop sometimes to block because if you used wooden ones, they'd swell during the hot and humid weather and affect the hat size.

Down at Lee we had our own block maker. When he knew he had to make something, he'd go out and look around, find a tree, and cut it down and soak it. From then on we'd keep them right in water, never set them out on the bench and let them dry; otherwise, they'd go in and out. In the summer it will expand and in the winter it'll contract. He'd make one by hand. He had a

drop down evenly; it would clump. When they came in, it was just like somebody greased your car. That grease was so heavy on it, you'd have to scrape it off.

DH: Did you clean it?

GR: We finally did, at the end, the last two or three years, we bought one dry-cleaning machine and we started to dry-clean the fur. It made all the difference in the world. When that grease got out, they were so fluffy. When we were here, we had ten dry-cleaning machines and we used to dry-clean every pound of fur that came in. That settled the problem. They used to come up, those people who make soap, because we had barrels of grease. It was really something. Then we really made nice hats.

You blow the fur. You mix it first and put it in a mixer and mix it, some hare and different grades, and then you run it through a blower that has four, eight, twelve sections. They used to blow the fur out. It had a

> *"I liked hatting. It was very interesting, you know—kept you on your toes. But I mean, I liked it. People said I'm crazy. But they say that hatters are crazy anyway."*

duplicator, he'd put that block on, and duplicate the same thing.

    Lee had the best finishing shop. Mallory's was all concrete. But Lee's, all the floors in Lee's front shop were 2x4s on edge with a maple floor on top. It used to absorb a lot of the moisture that otherwise would have gone into the hat.

DH: Would you use poplar for those hat blocks?

GR: No, we used to use mostly maple. I imagine there are other— In this area that's all I'm familiar with.

DH: How do you make a white hat?

GR: On this beaver that we have here [*pointing to hat*]. You know that beaver is bleached. I don't know how they're doing it down in Texas. They used to buy the pieces from the furriers—the pieces left over. We had a method. We finally found a method where we could dye the regular beaver without using the bleached beaver. That's why that's a nice hat. You see, when you get the bleached pieces, they loose their strength. We had a young fellow who used to work for us, not a chemist. He worked on it, so finally what we used to do was get the regular beaver (of course, take the grease out), and run it down to just the size before color and then we would bleach it, because otherwise you couldn't form it. Once we got it formed, we bleached it. Then we made some real nice hats.

    I liked hatting. It was very interesting, you know—kept you on your toes. But I mean, I liked it. People said I'm crazy. But they say that hatters are crazy anyway.

    There were many, many smaller hat companies in Danbury during the big production years. They were called jobbers and supplied unfinished bodies to smaller suppliers all over the country. Today only the big names are remembered, Lee, Mallory, Adams, and Stetson.

1. Danbury, Connecticut

Mallory Hat Company workers taking a break. Courtesy of the Danbury Museum and Historical Society.

The Danbury Scott-Fanton Museum and Historical Society was formed in 1947 to acquire, preserve, exhibit, and interpret New England's past, and particularly the heritage of Danbury. Located in downtown Danbury, the museum preserves the John and Mary Rider House (ca. 1875), the Dodd Hat Shop (ca. 1790), and the Charles Ives Birthplace, along with the modern exhibit building, Huntington Hall, which also contains the museum offices and research library.

The hatting exhibits displayed in the eighteenth-century Dodd Shop interpret the impact of one industry on an entire region and attempt to explain Danbury's progression from a one-industry town to a vital modern city closely allied to high technology.

To support the hatting industry, there developed silk mills, paper and box factories, tanneries and fur companies, machine works, and, ultimately, unions to protect the employees.

2

Gentlemen's Hatters and Their Hats: Knox, Dunlap, Cavanaugh, Dobbs, Bollman, Langenberg, and Borsalino

> "The U.S. had a population of eighty million people, and was making approximately four million dozen men's hats a year—fur felt, all fur felt. They were making almost forty-eight million men's hats a year with a population of eighty million men, women, and children. . . ."—Bob Doran, 1996

Major hat companies emerged through the talent and initiative of single experienced hatters. John B. Stetson named his company after himself, as did Charles Knox and Frank H. Lee, among others. Partners and family members joining the firm solidified and expanded the business, but the expertise of the hatter, determined to make "the best possible hat," epitomized the hat's reputation and subsequent sales. Some of these craftsmen served their local clientele by stylishly shaping hats from already formed hat "bodies" bought from larger companies, such as McLachlan in Danbury, Connecticut. Other hat makers expanded their neighborhood shops into factories and multiple storefronts, gaining in sales and reputation until they had garnered national, then international, recognition. Many of these hatters—Knox, Dunlap, Cavanaugh, and Dobbs—famous in the nineteenth century, remain as familiar names in the twentieth. This is the story of their success.

Charles Knox was a top hat maker. He had built a business from nothing in the 1830s and 1840s, and achieved prominence by the 1860s by producing a quality product. Not only did he make a sturdy hat, but he had a sense of style that enabled him to became a leader of men's fashionable headwear. In addition, he was a good citizen who looked after his workers as well as his customers.[1] As my mother-in-law repeatedly said to me of her husband's Knox hats, "These were the best hats you could buy. George went every year to Fifth Avenue to get his new hat. Knox was the best!" This opinion was based on a history of good craftsmanship and compelling advertising.

When Charles Knox was twelve, he emigrated

from Scotland with his younger sister, but instead of being dropped at the port of New York City, where their family lived, they were set ashore in Wilmington, Delaware. Charles and his sister, having no money, walked the one hundred and eighteen miles to New York City, eventually, accidentally, and quite luckily finding one of their sisters, who led them to their family. It was a large family and everyone worked. Consistent with the times, Charles was apprenticed to the then famous hatters, Leary and Company, at their store at 105 Broad Street. He received twenty-five dollars a year, a standard wage for a boy at that time. He did so well that when he finished his apprenticeship, he received $250 and was hired by the firm at a salary of ten dollars per week. Soon he became foreman.

Knox went out on his own in 1838, setting up shop at 110 Fulton Street near the corner of Nassau Street. The sign read "Knox, Hatter" but he called the shop "The Hole in the Wall." Fulton Street was bustling with sailors on their way to the waterfront—Knox sold a lot of caps between four and five in the morning. Soon Knox needed a larger store to handle the volume. This he found at 128 Fulton Street in what was called the Old Sun Building. His pattern was set: move to where the customers were and keep expanding. Hatters looked for prime locations where there was a "stream of fashionable traffic."[2] Broadway was the best area, but the rents were high. Undaunted, Knox negotiated for the building at 212 Broadway and Fulton Street and got it.

His business was now in the right location, but the building was too ramshackle for his use, so he tore it down and built a new one. The retail store was on the ground floor, with the hat factory occupying the upper floors.[3] When the building burned in 1865, it cost sixty thousand dollars to rebuild, but Knox didn't let this stop him, and he was operating again in four months. Throughout his life, from the day he walked with his sister those one hundred and eighteen miles to the day he died in 1895, Charles Knox was persistent.

His persistence centered on his concern for a qual-

An early Knox advertisement.

ity product. The shop in which his hats were sold was described as "a large room, elegantly fitted up, with black walnut cases, a crowd of polite clerks, and a large assortment of hats. Nothing but a good and fashionable article is offered for sale, and the customer goes away satisfied."[4]

He was also known as a hard worker. Every day when he came to his shop he attended both his customers and all the people working in the manufacturing departments on the upper floors of his building. Today we might call this micro-management, but men like Knox and John B. Stetson, hat makers themselves, wanted their staff to maintain the quality they had originally produced. Being trained in manufacturing, they knew how to solve any problem that might arise in the complex process of making and styling a fur felt hat. (Even today John Milano, who manufactures Justin brand hats, started from the ground up.)[5]

Knox's reputation was made not only by the quality of his felt, but also by his fashionable styling. He was said to have led the fashion trends in New York City, which at that time led the nation. In 1870, George

2. GENTLEMEN HATTERS AND THEIR HATS

P. Rowell wrote of Knox in his book, *The Men Who Advertise*, "In shape, proportion, lines, and trim, his hats seemed always to anticipate the style. And because of the fine materials, the skillful workmanship, and the special care exercised in their finishing, they *held* their style. As a fashion writer of that day put it, 'They show their style as long as worn.'"[6]

Many hatters set the price of the hat before it was made. Not Knox: he did the opposite. First he made the best hat he could make, and then he determined the price. Since not everyone could afford his top-line hat, he made a second-level hat. Again, he made the best hat possible from a less expensive grade of fur (hare instead of beaver or nutria). In this manner, he could live up to his motto, "One must be first in his line or stand aside."[7]

But quality alone did not get him business; Charles Knox knew how to advertise, and he used news stories about his business to his advantage. When he had to fight city hall and Commissioner Loew for removal of a bridge that blocked his storefront, he got mileage out of publishing, "I have fought the good fight but 'Hard Knox' laid me Loew."[8]

For all hatters it is good business to publicize who buys their hats. Knox made it known that he sold hats to Daniel Webster, Horace Greeley, Henry Clay, Abraham Lincoln, and eventually to all the presidents of the United States and dignitaries all over the world.[9] In the New York papers, where he advertised extensively, his ads were "short, pithy, popular, readable and attractive." They appeared in the special notice column and were often connected to a current topic or event. For example, "Not a man who wore Knox's hats during the earthquake in San Francisco had them shaken off."[10] Knox was a man with timing and a sense of humor.

Luckily for Charles Knox, he had a son who was interested in taking over the business. Col. Edward Knox used as his motto, "I move and progress."[11] His style of management was as efficient as his father's, but also a bit more in tune with the current trends. His first move was uptown to Fifth Avenue and Madison Square, the new fashion center, where Col. Knox kept himself and his hats in the news. He expanded to three New York locations, until health problems and a decline in business forced him to sell his interest in the company to new management in 1913. This was the end of the Knox lineage, but not the end of the Knox hat.

Robert Dunlap apprenticed with Knox and Company, also at age twelve, in 1857. He, too, was "bright and eager." Starting wages were three dollars per week, for which he swept the floors and laid the fires. He was quick to learn and had a knack for making a quality hat. The story goes that he asked for a raise and when Knox refused, he went out on his own (in 1865, the same year John B. Stetson set up his shop in Philadelphia). Dunlap specialized in producing a fine derby hat, a style that would become increasingly popular as the nineteenth century progressed. To broaden his market, for Knox sold derbies too, Dunlap marketed them

Robert Dunlap was a large space advertiser and believed in telling his sales story with pictures.

throughout the United States. But he was still in direct competition with Charles Knox, even to the point of vying for the same building at Fifth Avenue and Madison Square. Knox won that battle, but Dunlap also ended up with three stores in New York City.

Dunlap had a broad view of the hatting business. In addition to men's headwear, he developed a line of women's hats and did very well with them, demonstrating his business sagacity. He also realized that he needed to hire men who knew how to make hats, and who were determined to make better hats than anyone else. One engineer worked five years on dyes and the dying process in order to make blacker hats, the hat color most popular at the time. Dunlap's efforts paid off. Other hat manufacturers would wait for the seasonal "Dunlap style" to come out before finishing their Derbies. Salesmen ordered in quantities of five hundred to one thousand dozen without knowing the exact style because they had so much confidence in Dunlap's expertise.[12] Not only a good businessman, he was a congenial manager who, when making his factory visits, served beer to the men and ice cream to the women. He knew how to support his people to encourage their best efforts.

By 1900, Knox was established across the country with sales agents setting up departments in high-class clothing stores. Dunlap followed suit by setting up agencies in leading men's furnishing stores. Both asked the question, "How can we make finer hats and sell more of them?" Rivalry continued throughout Dunlap's lifetime.

After Dunlap's death, his business started to decline. Since both Knox and Dunlap were in a decline in 1918, the obvious answer was to join the two companies. Both hatters shared a common tradition for quality hat making, a respect for their workers, and a desire to sell hats nationwide, and they both had loyal followings. A count of hats in a Bankers Club cloakroom in New York City revealed that out of 1,020 hats, 510 were Knox and 200 were Dunlap (the rest were other brands).[13]

Before Knox and Dunlap merged in 1918, Knox was plagued by what were then called "shop calls." A worker who had a grievance could make a "shop call" to discuss the problem, which would stop all work. The Knox management, deciding to do something creative about the problem, set up the Knox Work Council. Instead of stopping work, grievances were sent to the council where they were promptly settled. The workers were also given access to the records of costs and sales, advertising, and style choices. They even voted to cut wages in 1921 in order to lower the price of their hats when competition drove down the price of hats. Worker input eventually spread to the merchants, whose advice was solicited on styles, grades, colors, and advertising for the products they had to sell.

A convention of Knox and Dunlap sales agents was first called in January 1922 for the purpose of discussing sales and marketing concerns. Would anyone come? the company worried, since the agents had to pay their own fare. That year, seventy-four agents attended; one hundred twenty-three attended in 1923, and nearly two hundred in 1924. They had serious problems to discuss. After World War I, soaring material and labor prices made it difficult to maintain the required quality. The company needed to simplify. In 1926 the Knox-Dunlap Company offered 9,820 different styles, sizes, and colors of soft felt hats alone.[14] The agents decided to cut the number down to six styles in ten colors each. This simplification kept the costs down, reducing the overall styles from ten thousand to two thousand with "feature" hats for each season. On May 1, 1926, these decisions resulted in the first common stock dividend issued since 1913. In addition, a research fund was established—it was time for science to replace guesswork.

All efforts, scientific or otherwise, could not keep the hatting industry from shrinking during the twentieth century. From the 1920s onward, the hat industry began to experience the gradual downsizing that led to the eventual amalgamation or closing of almost all of the original hat labels known in the United States. Today only a few continue to exist—Stetson, Resistol, Knox, and Dobbs—but they are produced by a single corporation, HATCO. Knox and Dunlap were eventually bought by Byer-Rolnick, which was in turn bought by The Hat Corporation of America, which was then bought by A. D.J. Caps, and finally Hat Brands, Inc. (currently named HATCO).

Other hatters whose history began in the mid-1800s eventually made their way into the HATCO conglomerate. James A, Knapp first established himself in Danbury, Connecticut, then moved to Norwalk. He had two partners, Andrew J. Crofut, an expert felt-stiffener, and Henry Gillam, an expert brim-curler. Together they built a large manufacturing company called Crofut & Knapp. It was through this company that a now more recognizable name surfaced, John J. Cavanaugh (famous for his Cavanaugh edge). Initially foreman for C. & K., he became general manager, and then president.

Rose and Harry Rolnick

In 1908 a line of hats was developed by ad man Robert A. Holmes. He created the Dobbs line in conjunction with H. DeWit Dobbs of Fifth Avenue. They too were quite successful. Cavanaugh joined their group in 1928, creating Cavanaugh-Dobbs, Inc., keeping Cavanaugh, Ltd. as a subsidiary.

In 1927 hat maker Harry Rolnick, known for his commitment to quality, joined with a young millionaire, E. R. Byer, who was looking for an investment opportunity. They formed Byer-Rolnick of Dallas, Texas, which created the Resistol hat. ("Resistol" meant "to resist all weather" or "resist oil and sweat.") Byer-Rolnick produced a full product line that included traditional dress and formal hats (the Bradford Line), dress bowlers and

fedoras (the Churchill line), and the wider brimmed, higher crowned western styles.

Despite the change in ownership, sales were still down. Consolidation was imminent. In 1932 the Hat Corporation of America (HCA) bought out Cavanaugh-Dobbs, making John Cavanaugh president. In the mid-sixties, Resistol acquired HCA, then based in Danbury, Connecticut. Resistol labels now included Resistol, Keven Andrew, Bradford, Churchill, Champ, Knox, Dobbs, and Cavanaugh.[15] Richard Albert, formerly a sales representative with Resistol, explains the various permutations that got the company where it is today:

> It often happens that companies run by families or their original owners, as they age, run out of management talent. This was the case with HCA. They sold to the Salesky Brothers in 1968. Their company was Koret of California. Joe Koret was the creator of the perma-press process, which made pleats in garments stay permanently. The process was making so much money in the pants and shirts area that they wanted to expand. They bought a rainwear company, Oxford Clothes, a sweater company, and Resistol Hats (HCA). They now had a complete men's division and kept it for eleven years. During that time HCA had a strike that lasted over a year. With the absence of its name products, such as Resistol, Knox, Cavanaugh, Champ [originally from Sunbury, Pennsylvania] and Dobbs, other manufacturers filled the gap. After the workers' strike, their market share of 70% to 80% went down to 50%. Stores that carried only HCA had to diversify in defense of another strike, reducing product, and resulting in customer dissatisfaction. Because of the complexity of the hat business (advertising, boxes, linings, sweat bands, and labor issues), production was not effective unless

there was a strong market demand. Labels were condensed. Resistol dropped the dress hats and became only a western product line, while Dobbs became "the men's dress hat."

In 1979 Koret, owned by the Salesky Brothers, decided to sell to the Levi Strauss Company. Koret didn't want a men's division anymore, only ladies'. By this time, Resistol had acquired the leasing of the Stetson label. (The Stetson company leases only its name; it had already sold its machinery to the Stevens Hat Company of St. Joseph, Missouri, in 1971). Levi Strauss was buying the Stetson name at the peak of the "Urban Cowboy" craze. That craze had a two-year lead, eased in with the increasing popularity of country-western music, Nashville, and line-dancing. Levi Strauss kept the hat division as a separate company with its own management team, which continued to market its product as usual; however, employees were able to receive Levi Strauss benefits, stock options, profit bonuses, and full medical coverage. Levi Strauss never really understood the complex production of hats. They were comfortable with the stamp-out process of making jeans that could be subcontracted all over the world. They sold the hat division to Irving Joel of A.D.J. Caps in 1985.

In 1982 Irving Joel owned A.D.J. Caps of Richmond, Virginia, and made a variety of caps. He was an aggressive merchant who loved the headgear business. First he bought Texas Miller, whose labels were Adam Hats, a popularly priced hat coupled with Bonds clothes (like the old J.C. Penny brands), and others.

Mr. Joel loved hats, and by 1985 he wanted more. Levi Strauss wanted to sell. So in the mid-eighties, Irving Joel bought the business for about fifty-five million dollars. In 1993 he sold it for approximately two and one-half times that amount. The investment company of Hicks and Muse put the Hat Brands package together: Dobbs, Resistol, lease of the Stetson label, and a limited contract with Biltmore of Canada. They added Lone Star Beer, A & W Rootbeer, and in 1992 Montana Silversmith and Charley One-Horse Hats.

At present, the challenge to Hat Brands is to move ahead with the old labels in place. They represent a diversity of styles, from the golf cap to the feather-decorated, spray-painted Charley One-Horse western hat. If the company or its employees are not able to abandon their old ideas, they need to change rapidly enough for the success of the company.[16]

One company that remained under family ownership from 1860 until 1992 was the Langenberg Hat Company of Washington, Missouri. Langenberg attempted employee ownership during the 1990s. When that failed, they were luckily bought by Jan Lewis of Texas, daughter of the founder of the American Hat Company in Conroe, Texas. Jan has now restored the Langenberg factory to its former manufacturing potential. American Hat Company produces only western style hats. Jan said that buying the Langenberg factory has added a multiethnic face to their product line. She loves the diversity, and the fun that this variety allows. She is also interested in tapping the talents of workers who have been in the hat making industry all their lives (some second- and third-generation hat makers). She said that this helps keep hat production and jobs in the United States. American Hat and the former Langenberg factory now produce a full line of dress and western hats.[17]

Roy Langenberg, last of the family line to run the company, said that Langenberg started in 1860 as a wholesaler, not as a manufacturer. At one time they were a large client of the Stetson Company, but by the early 1890s they started to manufacture their own line of hats. Langenberg emphasized that in 1910 over three million dozen fur felt hats were sold. The machine that made this possible was the former. The size of a company's production was determined by the number of forming machines it had in operation.[18]

A former operates when fur is blown onto an eighteen- to twenty-inch revolving copper perforated cone, which is then dipped into a hot soapy bath, and the fur expertly slipped from the mold. This is the first step in the felting process. After that, the cone is shrunk to approximately one-third its original size, ultimately reaching the stage where it is blocked into a man's fur felt hat.[19] In 1919, Stetson had fifty-two cone formers making men's dress hats (less than 5 percent at that time were western hats). Although Langenberg continued to make its own brand of hats, it also supplied many smaller firms and hat makers with unfinished hat bodies from which they styled their own labels.

Another independent company still in operation is the Bollman Hat Company in Adamstown, Pennsylvania. George Bollman started in 1868 in a partnership with Issac Sowers. The company was small and survived into the twentieth century chiefly by manufacturing women's headwear. In 1900, after his father's death, George W. Bollman joined the firm after having previously worked for Hendel Hat. George W. was able to clear the firm's debt and establish a partnership with his mother, who had inherited the factory, land, building,

Former. Photograph by John Brandwood.

and equipment. The business remained small, diversifying at times to keep the plant in operation year around. The Bollman Company specialized in wool felt, a commodity much endangered in the 1920s by Italian and Japanese imports, approximately 95 percent of the millinery bodies used in the U.S. As secretary of the Wool Hat Manufacturers Association, George W. Bollman was instrumental in getting the tariffs changed to curb foreign competition from countries that paid lower wages.[20]

The depression was good for Bollman. People could ill afford the more expensive fur felt hats, but needed to wear hats, so they turned to the less expensive wool felt supplied by Bollman. Business slowly expanded and a partnership was made under the name of Bollman Carbonizing Company. Buildings were added in 1936 and 1939 to accommodate the expansion of the carbonizing wool and wool noil division.

Hat companies did not always merge; sometimes, as in the case of Bollman and and Miller, they supported one another. Miller Brothers Hat Company was a large jobber and manufacturer that decided not to make or finish any more wool hat bodies. They asked Bollman to supply them, causing a 400 percent increase for Bollman.

The third generation of Bollmans took over in 1940 when George W. died. George W. had helped the firm to grow from sixty employees in 1900 to five hundred in 1940. The company was now one of the top five wool felt hat manufacturers in the United States. Five sons, all knowing the hatting business, joined the firm. The company was active during World War II making felt slippers and felt scopes for the Army. After the war, the company expanded in several directions. It divided into two corporations, and set up a research laboratory specializing in more efficient ways to scour (clean) the wool.

Sales dropped in 1947 with the "new look" for women, which featured defined waistlines and longer

Hat Making Apparatus Invented by John E. Kane, Danbury, Connecticut

Patented Sept. 5, 1944

#2,357,475

"This invention relates to the handling of fur and more particularly to an apparatus and a method for supplying fur to a bat-former cone to thereby form hat bodies or bats from the fur.

"An object of this invention is to provide apparatus for handling fur in a carefully controlled and efficient manner to form hat bats, for example upon perforated cones. Another object is to provide a method and apparatus for handling fur and the dividing of fur into predetermined amounts. A still further object is to provide a method and apparatus of the above character for supplying fur in predetermined quantities to the cones of a bat-former in a dependable and efficient manner. A further object is to provide apparatus of the above character for receiving bulk fur and producing from this fur bats of standard high quality and of proper size and weight. Another object is to provide apparatus which is compact and sturdy in construction and efficient and dependable in operation."

from patent application dated July 8, 1940

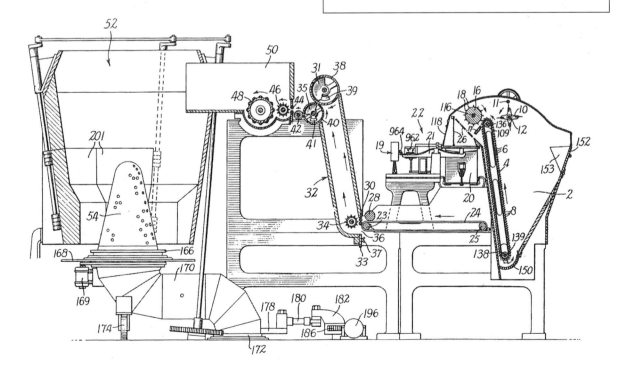

skirt lengths. By 1954 there were only five wool felt manufacturers left. When the Merriman Hat Company in Amesbury, Massachusetts, decided to sell, the Bollman Company bought them out. "In 1954, the company produced 155,000 dozen ladies' bodies, representing 28% of the total industry. In 1955, with the Merriman business, this production nearly doubled to a 52% industry share. The men's wool felt hat business jumped in market share from 22% to 40%."[21]

Research continued during the late 50s and early 60s, as did improved sales and manufacturing techniques. But the 1960s hit all hat manufacturers hard. Bollman was a key employer in Adamstown, and the Bollman brothers wanted to make some plans to continue this position, at the same time responding to the downtrend in sales. They were able to sell the business to five key employees in April 1974. Dan Bollman, grandson of the founder, said, "The company's niche was producing the best quality product in the business and still remaining competitively priced."[22] Bollman continues today to be employee-owned and produces a line of wool felt hats for both men and women and fur felt hats for the winter season.

Borsalino shop in Alessandria, Italy.

Borsalino

The Borsalino name is as recognizable as Stetson. In their 1999 advertising brochure they describe Borsalino as making hats for "the most creative, sophisticated classes of today's Italian society. . . . Borsalino means tradition and a modern approach, class and functionalism, style and practicality. It is the symbol of a thoroughly Italian tradition that has proved its ability to make its mark on style all over the world and keep up with the times."[23]

The Borsalino factory building still stands in the center of Alessandria, Italy, even though it is now not the source of the famous Borsalino hat. In order to modernize production and distribution, the hat maker moved to an industrial park on the outskirts of the city, leaving their old factory to be converted into the local university and a hat museum.[24]

As with other individual hat makers, Giuseppe Borsalino started in his own small shop after an apprenticeship in Paris at the Maison Berteil. By 1900 the small atelier had enlarged to an operation employing one thousand workers and producing a million hats. This was the era when all hat makers were doing big business. Borsalino had imported the most avant-garde English machinery, which added to the efficiency of their efforts toward making a quality hat. By 1910 they produced two million hats, and with customers like the royal family, the wearing of a Borsalino became a symbol of status.[25] Since then Borsalinos have been custom ordered by the stars—Bruce Willis, Michael Jordan, and Roberto Benigni, among others.

The company continued as a family-run business through Giuseppe's oldest son, Teresio, and then his grandchild, Teresio Usuelli. By the one-hundredth anniversary of the founding of the company, the Borsalino facilities were counted among the largest in their sector of Europe.[26]

Again, as with the other hat manufacturers, the second half of the twentieth century saw a decline in hat wearing, resulting in consolidations and closings. Borsalino continued until the Gallo-Monticone family of Asti bought the firm in 1992. Their goal is to continue to seek worldwide markets and a diversification of product lines.

To help accomplish this, in 1998 Borsalino established a distributor in Manhattan to promote its hats in the United States, Mexico and the Caribbean countries. Borsalino is also organizing a factory in China to produce articles for the Far Eastern markets. Further licensing agreements and separate pricing of new or similar

Salesman demonstrating the shaping and wearing of the primo Borsalino hat, the Icaro, in the Alessandria shop.

The variety of Borsalino felt fedoras.

products, not with the traditional logo, are part of the expansion. The company has already expanded into fragrances, ties, umbrellas, scarves, caps, and leather goods, making hats a small part of the accessory business. "Quality, hand-craftsmanship, timeless elegance, and an 'international' vocation have made Borsalino a worldwide market leader with sales amounting to more than 19 million Italian Lires in 1998 (up by about 20% over 1997)."[27] To handle future growth in Asia a 1998 agreement was made with Aurora of Tokyo for production, distribution, and licensing of the range of Borsalino products in Japan and the entire Far East.

A new line of particular interest is the *Icaro,* their lightest available felt, weighing a mere 48 grams. It is made of the absolutely best fur available, comes in a range of colors, and is truly crushable, which makes it a favorite for travel. One reason for the longevity of Borsalino's success is their ability to combine classic styles with a slightly new shape. The *Como,* with its 2½-inch brim, is their best seller in the United States. It also comes in a wide range of colors. In fact, Borsalino is known for its colors—sixty different colors, including reds, blues, greens, and yellows—far beyond the standard grays, browns, and tans.

A line of women's hats was added in the mid-1990s. All these can be found in their own shops in Alessandria, Milan, Florence, Rome, Bari, Asti, and Bologna, where classic felt hats, Panamas, and Monticristis abound. In the United States, stores such as Saks Fifth Avenue, Bergdorf Goodman, Nieman Marcus, and Barneys maintain a steady supply. Some of the specialty hat shops around the county also stock Borsalino straws and felts. And yes, there is always the Internet.

One other European company, Tonak, is located in the Czech Republic. Tonak has been in operation since 1799, and continues to produce a full range of fur felt hats.[28]

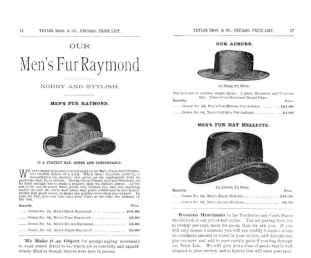

The Homburg

by John Wm. McMicking, Hat Maker

Simply put, if we consider the original soft felt Alpine Hat that became known in the 1880s as the "Fedora" as being the ancestor of the modern Fedora and the ancestor of the modern Homburg (as well as that of the Trilby, "Porkpie," and "Crusher"), then we can see that all of these soft felt hats are variations of that original "Fedora" rather than hats with separate and distinct origins.

In the same way that the Top Hat of 1900 was simply an everyday hat and was not elevated to a level of ceremonial formality until the end of the nineteenth and the beginning of the twentieth centuries, and in the same way that the Bowler was simply an early protective hard hat for gamekeepers in 1850 and was not raised to formality until the 1920s or later, the "Homburg" that was made popular by Edward VII as Prince of Wales was an extremely casual hat without any hint of formality to it at all. In the 1890s (though the date of the Homburg may be in question—1860s, says Fiona Clark) it was the prince's wearing of this hat that made it fashionable and, hence, copied by would-be social climbers. [The "new fangled" silk Top Hat was not considered an acceptable replacement for the traditional Beaver Top Hat until Prince Albert, the Prince Consort, wore one to the Great Exhibition of 1851 (or so the story goes) and the Bowler Hat, which H.M. King George V wore, but never "in town," was not raised to a level of royal fashion, and thus to be copied, until Edward VIII as Prince of Wales (in the 20s and early 30s) chose to wear one upon occasions for which his father would have seen only a Top Hat as acceptable.]

The rise in acceptability of the soft felt hat (Homburg/Fedora/Trilby) for wear in town or city did not really occur until the shellac shortage experienced during the First World War prevented hat makers from making their usual quantity of stiff felt hats (Bowlers/

Cambridges). The number of male heads that did not march off to war still exceeded the number of stiff felt hats that could be made, so there was no choice but to make soft felts available to men who would have previously worn Bowlers. The war saw a decline in standards and a loss of traditions; the hat-wearing public had experienced the comfort and convenience of the soft felt hat, so after the war there was no great rush to buy previously unavailable stiff felt Bowlers. Much of what was not acceptable before the war was now acceptable (a loosening of morals, less rigidity in manner of dress—frock coats gave way to cutaway morning coats which in turn gave way to the lounge suit, essentially, the present-day three-piece business suit) and there was a greater demand for and expectation of comfort than pre-war societal dictates had allowed.

As the twentieth century progressed the Bowler, which had all but replaced the Top Hat, soon reached its highest level of formality and was often seen as too formal for even the rising middle class. The next hat down in order of formality, the Homburg, was the obvious choice for the man who felt that the Bowler was too formal (or just old-fashioned). The Homburg had the ribbon-bound rolled brim edge of the Bowler and the older and not "ultraformal" Top Hat, but it was made of softer, more comfortable felt (though it has been rightly observed that a well-made, properly fitting Bowler is just as comfortable as any soft felt hat) and the soft felt crown could be dented or battered without fear of cracking the felt.

It was not until the 1940s and later that the Homburg began to be seen as a "formal" hat and was, subsequently, produced from a stiffer felt befitting its new formal (or, at least, semi-formal) status. It was not as stiff as a Bowler, but it was no longer as soft as it had been. The Second World War brought many changes and, as was the case with the First World War, society saw another decline in standards and a further loss of traditions. When Eisenhower chose to wear a black Homburg to his 1953 Inauguration instead of the traditional black silk Top Hat, old ways were abandoned and a casual hat that was originally thought appropriate only for rural use was elevated to a new level of presidentially sponsored formality.

Sir Anthony Eden (Chamberlain's foreign secretary in 1935, Churchill's deputy prime minister in 1951, and prime minister from 1955 to 1957) was a popular public figure in post-war Britain who was always regarded as stylishly well tailored and almost invariably topped off his Savile Row suits with a black Lock & Co. Homburg. As a result the Homburg (sometime renamed the "Anthony Eden") rose in popularity and became acceptable for use in situations that before the war would have required a Bowler. And, thus, the Homburg replaced the Bowler much in the same way that the Bowler replaced the Top Hat.

Homburgs were worn low and straight across the forehead, as this unknown gentleman illustrates.

Homburgs were produced in a variety of colors. Black was the choice for formal, business and sombre occasions, while grays and shades of brown from light to dark were the more fashionable choice for "day wear."

In short, an extremely casual hat which became fashionable in the second half of the nineteenth century because of a "royal connection" rose in popularity and perceived formality as a result of a shellac shortage at the beginning of the twentieth century, a steady decline in social standards (which characterized the twentieth century), and the hat-wearing public's desire for the greater comfort afforded by a soft felt hat.

With the decline in hat wearing from the 1960s to the present day (hats worn for sun protection being the primary exception) hats of any kind were thought of as old-fashioned; out of style; from a previous age—worn by old men and eccentrics. And now, in the early years of the twenty-first century the Homburg, like the Bowler and the Top Hat (and virtually any other type or style of hat), is generally regarded as a theatrical piece of period costuming usually found in a box on the shelf next to the spats and starched collars. *O Tempora! O Mores!*

2. Gentlemen Hatters and Their Hats

Conversation with Robert (Bob) Doran

October 19, 1996, Scott-Fanton Museum, Danbury, Connecticut

Bob Doran had an intimate relationship with the fur hat industry. He was the last in the line of one hundred twenty years of Doran Bros., a company that produced hat making machinery. He was a salesman who knew the business inside and out, traveling to hat manufacturers all over the world, selling and representing Doran Bros.

Mr. Doran began this interview by explaining the history of cloth. Early Egyptian pictographs show workers separating fibers with bows. Felt is perhaps the oldest type of continuously used fabric, and is still used in the making of the man's felt hat. The finest furs are desired, and were separated from the guard hairs by the bowing technique up to about 1845. The large bow was plucked by hand to create an air current that formed a loose cone shape that the hatters kneaded by hand into felt. The hatter could make five or six hats a day.

In 1845 the Wells and Burr Forming Machine was invented. This machine blew the fur onto a perforated cone under which an exhaust fan held the fur in place. These early formers could make thirty dozen hats a day.

DH: Stockport still has some of these forming machines in their hatting museum.

RD: These are modern. Now many types of felting machines developed. They all were roller mechanisms. Some were slats unevenly spaced on rollers to push and pull the material and provide the felting motions. Some had spiral wound rope on opposing rollers creating the necessary action to make the fibers move and shrink. When forming and felting became mechanized, further machines developed in the United States and Europe for all other operations: coloring, blocking crowns and brims, surface finishing, etc.

The industry after about 1850 moved from a craft operation to large factories employing hundreds of people and making up to 1500 dozen hats a day—completely finished hats. Now that was the beginning of the fur felt hat industry. You had your peak from the development of the forming machine up until about the turn of the century. This was in the United States and Europe. The fur hatting industry never developed as such in Asia. In the U.S. in 1903 the men's hat industry made three and one-half to four million dozen men's hats with a population of about eighty million people. They had about 350 formers operating in the U.S. in 1900. Machinery development peaked out with few exceptions in the 1930s and 40s. The decline in hat consumption had

Bob Doran

"*I'm the last of 120 years of the hatting industry—living with household talk, and knowing all those people. This has always been our company, with contacts with our customer s all over the world.*"

made a negative economic climate.

DH: What is your relationship to the hatting industry?

RD: I'm the last of 120 years of it—living with household talk, and knowing all those people. This has always been our company, with contacts with our customers all over the world.

DH: Tell me about the Failsworth Company.

RD: Failsworth was the biggest hat company in the world. Failsworth, at the end of World War II, had twenty-four forming machines operating. That's twenty-four machines at fifty dozen hats a day. They were the largest individual hat manufacturer in the world. Some of the literature says they had thirteen, but that was in their English plant. They had more in Dunedin, Scotland.

When you talk about England, and the disintegration of the English hat industry, you have a unique situation. England had a massive hat industry in relation to its domestic population. When the U.S. had two hundred formers, England had one hundred forty-two, and we had double their population. But before World War II, the English hatters were supplying basic hats to their Empire. What happened, you see—in all the phases of the Empire and the other countries they were exporting hats to, there were smaller hat manufacturers—felt hat manufacturers. But when World War II came along, England was out of the hat business for six years. So all of these companies in the satellite dominions, if they wanted hats, they had to make their own. The industry in Australia blossomed, and the industry in New Zealand blossomed, and the industry in South Africa blossomed—all around the world. In South America there was a huge market for English production. That all became self-sustaining. The war ended. England had these massive plants and all of a sudden, they had no more customers, through no fault of their own, or lack of imagination, or merchandising. It was just an act of history. But up until that point these were very, very big, shrewd operations, and they were just as thoroughly mechanized.

History gets distorted. People make the statement that all the machinery used today is one hundred years old. That's completely fallacious because fur felt machinery didn't actually start until after the Well's Former started (and could do thirty dozen a day). That's when

2. Gentlemen Hatters and Their Hats

Doran Brothers, Danbury Connecticut, in 1968, its hundredth anniversary

Taylor and Danbury realized—we have to have machines. That's when the Taylor machines and multi-rollers developed. Have you heard of Apron settlers?
DH: No.
RD: They're another type of slat machine on a belt. If you feed the bodies in, they impart motion in felting. There were basic hat machinery companies. Taylor was one of the first in the U.S. on a big scale. Wells developed the former about 1845, which made the thirty dozen a day. Now that same former was invented, patented, and sent all around the world. All the world adopted the Wells-type former. All the world had been using the bow up to that point, and now it just exploded! After the Industrial Revolution in basic textiles, the hat business was left completely behind, except for the blower.

It was sixty years later that the Industrial Revolution hit the fur hat business with all kinds of machinery. Our [Doran Bros.] date was 1868. Turner Atherton was in Stockport, England; they were in the 1860s. Oldham Sons were in England. They started the same year we did, 1868. They made multi-roller felting machines. In Germany you had Heinz. Heinz was mammoth. They supplied all the needs of all of Europe at the time, and most of the rest of the world. They were ingenious inventors. There were a lot of Heinz machines in the United States. And they made everything from fur cutting machines, all the way through to the finishing machines.
DH: When did the hat industry peak?
RD: It peaked in 1903. The U.S. had a population of eighty million people, and was making approximately four million dozen men's hats a year—fur felt, all fur felt. They were making almost forty-eight million men's hats a year with a population of eighty million. In Europe we had the mechanization of all these machines: formers, blowers, the different types of high-speed felting machines, the different brim stretchers to break out the crown, the blocking machines to get the rough blocking shape to the finish block. These all came in progression—roughly after 1860. New developments were coming along up until the late twenties, early thirties. Labor was still intensive, so each step in our company was—how do we take ten men off this job and do it with one machine?

Here's a very typical example—the Genest

Sicama multiroller.

machine. Back in the 1920s they took the multi-rollers out of business. It came into production in 1924. The Genest machine made a complete departure from the multi-roller system. Homer Genest was a very clever mechanical engineer working for the American Founders Company in Rhode Island, making cigarette machinery—very sophisticated machinery. They were commissioned by a group of Danbury hatters, Frank Lee and Harry McLachlan, to develop a new type of felting machine that would work faster and take fewer people than the multi-rollers and Taylor-types, and Genest was working on his car back in the twenties when cars still had running boards, and running boards were kind of slippery. When you stepped off one in the rain, your foot would slip and you'd fall and break your neck. So early on, they developed a piece of rubber with a series of lumps and bumps on it to give you traction. Genest was putting in a new piece of rubber material—like an amateur carpet layer—so that when you push one way you get a lump. All of a sudden, he started looking at these little bumps. Every time he'd push it, these little bumps would wiggle. He thought, here we have some very simple, independent motions. Can we apply these motions to felt? So he built two different types, molded into continuous belts with bumps on them. He would run the hat body through a series of rollers. As the hat body went over the roller, the bumps would change. So now you had thousands of little rubber fingers moving back and forth, independent of every other little rubber finger, each moving on its own, as they go over and under, rollers opening and closing. You push a hat body through there and all these little fibers were being massaged.

It was such a basic machine they didn't sell it;

2. GENTLEMEN HATTERS AND THEIR HATS

> "*Felt is the culmination of the migration of individual fibers in a random mass. All other textiles are a product of animal or vegetable fibers that are first spun or twisted into a thread or yarn which is then woven, knitted, or otherwise mechanically made into a fabric.*"

they rented it. The U.S. became almost a total Genest felting operation because each machine saved something like twenty people. They made one basic mistake in renting their machines because they rented them by the month instead of by the piece produced. So what happened was—the hatters immediately decided to run the machines three shifts. The contract didn't say how many hours. With their patents they could just as easily have made it per piece and made ten times as much money. Europe never went that way except here and there because their labor costs weren't that high.

Now technically, the multi-rollers and the refined type felting rollers gave felting a better quality product. So in the U.S. they would all have a few multi-rollers in their system. Actually, the felting had to be done in two stages in the Genest machine. One would bring the cones halfway to size, and then they would dye them so they would accept the dye. Then they would go in another type Genest machine with the same basic principle and felt them the rest of the way down. But then they'd leave the last half-inch or quarter-inch on their better quality hats, and do those in the multi-roller machines because the multi-roller motion was more sympathetic to what the fibers wanted to do.

DH: What exactly is felting?
RD: In a wool or rabbit fur the fibers are keratin, a substance whose outer walls are overlapping scales. When any motion is imparted to the edge of the overlap, the fiber moves in the direction of its root end; the direction of motion is an imperative of the angularity of the overlap—a ratchet effect.

When motion is applied to a completely random disposition of fibers, each fiber in the mass begins to move in its *root* direction; in motion the fibers collide, loop around in the mass and keep moving until all avenues of movement are blocked off and the mass has become a completely locked in nondirectional fabric. This is felt.

It is the culmination of the migration of individual fibers in a random mass. All other textiles are a product of animal or vegetable fibers that are first spun or twisted into a thread or a yarn which is then woven, knitted, or otherwise mechanically made into a fabric.

In making a fur felt hat, you have to keep the fibers felting—I mean, you have to keep the fibers moving in their own natural direction, at their own pace. In any of these operations, even by hand, if you try applying too much power or too much speed, you begin what we call "pushing" the fibers or "shoving." This is pushing the fibers faster than they are inclined to move on their own. It could cause lumps because the fiber is not moving of its own accord now. It's being shoved or

> "*Because of the craft nature of making hats, it does not relate to any other textile industry. No other sources had to learn 'hands on.' Even when people went to college, they had to learn in the industry.*"

pushed. Once you have formed a hat, when you get into the finishing operations, when you get to the abrasive operations with the sandpaper, when you begin to work your way into the surface to develop the smooth outside finish—all of a sudden, these things show up. You'll have a bump or a rough spot, or what we call a "push" or "shove" mark, and then you have a piece of junk. You can't make it right. It may look simple, but it isn't. It has to be timed to the individual fiber in the random mass of fibers. You can augment by lubrication of the fibers. They move a little bit faster, but you can't go beyond the critical ability of the fiber to accept its own motion, otherwise you're creating a bad situation in the body of the felt.

In these felting operations you run across the term *crozing*. When the loose fibers are first dipped into hot water, before being peeled off the cone, you get a heat shock that make the fibers jerk together. That gives them a mechanical bond. Now you start your different rolling operations. You have an outside and an inside, it will felt together. What you do is, after a certain number of passes, you take the hat body and rotate it—that's called crozing. After so many passes, you croze it, and after many other passes, you turn it inside out and continue the operation.

The reason you do that is because all the motions are being imparted from the outside of the material, so the fibers nearest the motion get the first work, so they are tightening up faster and more cohesively than the fibers inside the mix. So when you're turning it inside-out, you're tightening the fibers inside as well as outside, keeping them equal. No matter how carefully you felt, the fibers on the surface are more tightly felted than the core material. This is important when you get into the finishing operations, when you use abrasive sandpaper to generate the surfaces. You can't sand inside of that top layer. If you do, you have a problem because you have a different consistency of fabric in the sandwich, so you must stay on top of the crust. The finishing operations—your sandpapering, greasing, and powdering—must all take place without getting into the body.

The Doran Bros. Co. concentrated on the finishing operations. In later years we bought the Genest Company because they were going out of business. It was a free pickup for us.

Blocking machinery came along in the late 1800s, early 1900s. Before then all the blocking had been done by hand. You put the hat body in boiling water, and pulled it on a wooden shape. The mechanical blocking machines are very sophisticated machines because the hat is an oval. All of those fingers have to be on the same oval as the oval of the hat. They all have to be pulling at the same ratio against the center point of that

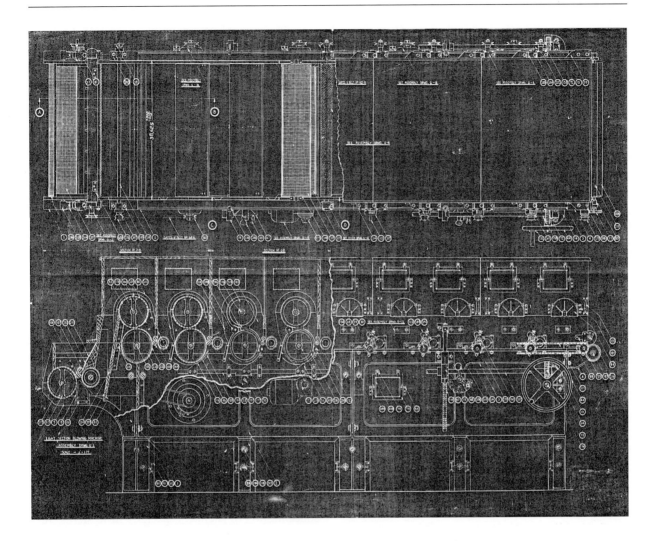

hat to get a stable brim, and to establish a basic crown line. Now you're going to do some other interesting operations to finish the hat. You're finishing with high-speed sandpaper—you call them jiggers. In making a crown jigger, you must keep the oval shape of the hat from bouncing from the center drive. This is the first pouncing operation on the rough hat body just after it has been formed with a rough crown and brim. Now this is a very high-speed sandpaper operation. You have a continuous sandpaper belt that goes around the crown. You have a comparable machine that does the brim. Pouncing is a French word, *pouncer,* for shaving. In England and northern Europe it's called shaving—pouncing in France. You go pretty fast, but there is a limit to how fast you can go. This is the telling operation of all finishing because it involves friction heat. Previously, the hat has been sized with liquid shellac—in the crown and brim of the hat to give it stiffness. The trick is to get penetration of the shellac below the surface for it to be an integral part of the hat. The first pouncing is not too critical. With finish pouncing, the sandpaper is mechanically fed over a rubber pad, using fresh sandpaper for each hat to get a uniform finish. Now the machine is set with a dimension of the oval shape hat. To compensate for the oval of the hat, the drive shaft of the machine has a double oval throw-in that cancels out the oval from the center of the shaft down the left side of the machine, and doubles the oval on the right side.

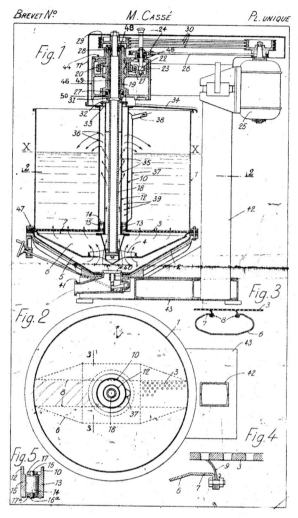

Pressure Dyeing Machine
Marcel Cassé, Soemac, Essane, France

This dyeing machine was used when the hats were in their final cone size. Dyeing was slow because of the tightness of the felt, which required a long exposure to the dye to get an even color. Europe used this method because "felting" was a fairly continuous process in the multi-roller system; it was impractical to interrupt the process when the cones were only partially felted to get easier penetration. In the United States, where the Genest A and B machines were used for felting, it was practical to dye at the halfway stage betwen A and B. The felt was not so tight, and penetration was fast and thorough in simple tumble dyeing machines.

So now your tool can work the left side of the oval without bouncing and digging in and out of the side of the hat. That gives an evenness of control against the hat. The pouncing paper itself has almost a line contact with the felt. This machine runs at 3,600 strokes per minute, producing a lot of heat that could burn the shellac. The key to pouncing is determining how fast you can jig the tool to generate the cutting speed and the pressure you need, against the balance of generating heat that will burn the shellac. If it burns, it comes out as a white stain. Now the pressure is regulated by a series of cams and springs. As the tool works around the hat, the exposure to surface area is always changing. When hitting the tip of the hat, you use just a touch effect, with minimum pressure. As it swings across the flat, the big surface exposure, there is an increase of pressure and slowing speed. Then, crossing the square area between crown and brim on top, pressure is released; then, down the side, pressure increases, etc. This is an all-automatic-speed hydraulic mechanism. The pressure is adjusted by cams and springs. The machine is adjusted to the depth of the crown you are putting on. To compensate for the oval, four speed changes per revolution are required. When into the brim, where there is a heavy concentration of shellac, especially in westerns (real heavy concentration), it gets trickier. You think it's easy because it's a flat surface, but it's not a flat surface. A hat has scope, the arc. Every machine this hat goes into has to conform itself to the arc or scope, one-eighth to one-quarter inches in depth.

After the hat is blocked, you iron the crown and brim, because in the steam blocking you have pulled the felt loose. The hats are wet when put on there. You reshrink the surface to a degree that has been destroyed by the blocking—the crown and brim irons do that. The brim iron looks like a simple thing. You have the brim on this very sophisticated drive spindle, moving up and down—flat iron for the bottom, heavy iron for the top. This little iron is to augment and tighten up the ninety-degree angle at the band line. The scope is compensated

Fur felt Homburg

> OUTLINE OF HAT MAKING
> (as used at Lee's)
>
> **Fur Shop Operations**
> 1. Purchase skins
> 2. Tumble to soften and remove fat
> 3. Tumble to remove sawdust
> 4. Slit and remove legs
> 5. Carrot
> 6. Dry
> 7. Stretch
> 8. Cut fur
> 9. Blow to remove heavy pieces
>
> **Back Shop Operations**
> 10. Mix (conical and 2 cylinders)
> 11. Blow to remove hair
> 12. Form
> 13. Wetting on the form cone
> 14. Hardening
> 15. Starting
> 16. Genest "A"
> 17. Dry
> 18. Size marks
> 19. Dyeing
> 20. Genest "B"
> 21. Tip Stretching
> 22. Brim Stretching
> 23. Water Blocking
> 24. Dry
> 25. Brim Stiffening
> 26. Short Dry
> 27. Rough Crown Pouncing
> 28. Rough Brim Pouncing
> 29. Vacuum Cleaning
>
> **Front Shop Operations**
> 30. Blocking
> 31. Crown Ironing
> 32. Brim Ironing
> 33. Crown pouncing
> 34. Crown Greasing
> 35. Crown Ragging
> 36. Brim Pouncing
> 37. Brim Greasing

by the wiggle-waggle of the drive spindle.

Brim finishing is sanding 7200 strokes a minute. The brim is going through there with only three-sixteenths of an inch in contact with the sandpaper at about three and one half seconds per revolution. It has time to be air cooled, worked and cooled, worked and cooled, so you don't burn your shellac. These are some of the subtleties.

The rounding machine cuts the final brim. It sounds simple, but again it's an oval. You have to hold the hat with an expansion chuck that opens and closes in an oval motion. Most hats, when the brim is cut, are not even—wider in front, or back, or the side. It takes five cam plates in a rounding machine and these can be changed to the particular dimension of the required factory brim dimension. Rollers are used here to follow the plate—a cam.

The Cavenaugh brim edge is the most expensive. Hat Corporation of America developed this brim edge. When the body is off the forming machine when starting to felt, the edge is turned over and sewn with a chain stitch. Through all the felting operations this stitch is retained. Once felted, you pull out the stitch. This is very expensive and labor intensive because you must maintain the exact dimension from here to here—center of crown to edge of brim.

Do you know why the bow is on the left side? It is a hangover from decades when there was trailing ornamentation on the hat that hung down. It had to be on the left side to free the sword arm.

Originally all hats were made round. It wasn't until after the Civil War that they began to make hats in an oval shape. All were round and made in three sizes— L, M, S—so you had a drawstring. The reason that stays there today is that you need a center line for all trimmings. You have to relate to one place on your object. When blocking or pressing, the machine leaves a little dimple, marking the exact center of the back at the bottom of the band line. Now when you come to put trims on the hat, you have that center line as your reference point.

The hand finisher was the prince of the hat making operation. Even during the depression a hand finisher could make up to $100 a week when in 1930, 1931, a normal working man could bring home $20 per week. This was the man we put out of work with our machines. All of our machinery did the work that he so skillfully did by hand, and we could actually do it better. He hand-sanded. He was an artist. I'm serious. This was very artistic work. He had to blend in that hat so all surfaces looked exactly the same—the crown and the brim—everything had to be done with his eye and his hand. Our machine had all the operations controlled as to pressure, speed, surface contact, and could do it consistently all day long with one completely unskilled worker. One person could run four machines and do one hundred and sixty dozen hats a day.[29]

Because of the craft nature of making hats, it does not relate to any other textile industry. No other sources had to learn "hands on." Even when people went to college, they had to learn in the industry. They would go to other hat factories in the world where their families were friends, and be exposed to all the other techniques, and they would do the same with their children. You had to learn it in a "hands-on" way, which made for a very tight-knit community. Everybody knew everybody on a personal basis and they were all engaged in this "ancient and mysterious art of felt making," as the first Queen Elizabeth called it. It was this unique set of circumstances that gave everyone that common bond. These people [hat manufacturers] competed on a national and international basis, but they liked to still know what each other was doing to a degree to enhance their own position. Some of them thought they had secrets, but they didn't. And, of course, being machinery manufacturers, we were privy to all their so-called secrets. The secrets would be that this guy would do this operation before the next operation, and this guy would do it in reverse.

Hat Corporation, Lee, and Stetson were the three biggest companies in the country at that time.

Italian law required patenting of machinery with the possibility of a ten-year extension beyond the first five if you could exhibit your machine in the Milan or Bari Trade Fair. In order to do this once, Doran Bros. got the Alderson Sons Co. sales rep for Doran Bros. in Europe to send a crated machine to the Trade Fair. They bribed a janitor to place it in an aisle, and were able to get their Italian patent extension.

DH: How much fur did it take to make a hat?
RD: One rabbit skin yielded approximately one ounce of fur and you needed four ounces per dress hat. If your forming machine produced six hundred hats a day, that meant 2,400 skins. In 1946 six hundred formers were operating in the world, which meant 1,440,000 skins per day or 316,800,000 skins per year (220 work days). Nineteen hundred three was the largest felt hat year, with probably about 600,000,000 skins used.
DH: Where did all of those rabbit skins come from?
RD: They came from Australia, Europe, and Asia. In Australia rabbits were introduced around 1800. The population grew to the hundreds of millions by the mid to late century with six hundred million by the 1950s.

> **Lee Back Shop Production**
>
> Hardening
>   Hand Former—50 doz. / 8 hr. $\frac{480}{50}$ = 9.6 min
> Starting
>   45 doz. / 8 hr. / 2 men $\frac{480}{22.5}$ = 21.1 min
> Genest A
>   20 hats / 12 min $\frac{12 \times 12}{20}$ = 7.2 min
> Genest B
>   3 doz. / 20 min. / 1.5 men $\frac{20 \times 3}{3 \times 2}$ = 10.0 min.
>
>   47.9 min
>
> *Bob Doran, September 1, 1950*

There are three hundred million today. In Europe and Asia the rabbits are wild, a food source, and the skins become available for the hat makers. White rabbits, albinos, are domestically bred for the white fur to be used in garments and hats that are dyed pastel colors.

DH: Was there any impact by Kennedy's not wearing a hat?

RD: No. Newspaper writers looking for a story and the hatters who didn't want to look at reality wanted to blame somebody—anybody—but Kennedy had nothing to do with it.

Again, the automobile and the spreading out of the population generated a more informal type of clothing, and a lot of the conventional things when we were young just went by the boards. You just didn't dress that way anymore.

DH: Does Hollywood influence the styles?

RD: Not really. Hollywood is a follower in men's clothing. It follows the trends. Hollywood couldn't be too far out because it couldn't be offensive to the mom and pop type of audience.

DH: What happened to the Doran Bros. Company?

RD: We finally sold the business in 1989, and now we're all retired.

3

The System of Hatmaking: Stetson, Resistol, and Stevens Hat Companies

"Machines Required for the United States Hat Production: Conical mixer, cyl. mixer (double units), blower, feeder (cyl. mix, blow), formers, hardening, starting, Genest A (to 14x23, 1½ dz.-14 min.), Casse (at Lee, 14 x 23 to 12½ x 18), dye kettles (250 dz.-2 hrs.), Genest B (3 dz.-20 min.), tip stretcher, brim stretcher (2 machines), wet block (2 machines), centrifugal dryer (2 units), stiffener, rough crown pounce (10 sec.), rough brim pounce, vacuum, blocking, cording, crown ironing, brim ironing, crown pouncing, crown greasing, crown ragging, brim pouncing, brim greasing, brim ragging, finisher speed lathe, pressing, curling."—Robert Doran, February 1, 1949

The twentieth-century hat industry has experienced as many changes as the eighteenth century's. In 1858 it was written that "the entire system of manufacture has been imperceptibly but effectually revolutionized." The widespread use of machinery "has silently brought about a transfer of the work from small shops to large factories, several stories high, in which all parts of the manufacture are carried on under the same roof, each floor being devoted to a separate portion of the work, which is conducted in a manner similar to the factory system of other countries, and of our large cotton centers."[1] The twentieth century saw the reversal—the multi-building complexes in Danbury, Philadelphia, Brooklyn, St. Joseph, Missouri, Guelph, Ontario, and Stockport, England—absorbed and discarded, forced, because fewer men were wearing hats, to reduce their production, tear down their buildings, and sell equipment to the remaining consolidators.

For a little over one hundred years, hat factories as large as small towns—and servicing their employees in a like manner—formed, finished, shipped, sold, and set the styles of men's headwear. The stories included in this book are from the men who spent their lives making and selling hats. Some of the stories are about the building of the companies; some are about their demise. Gary Rosenthal is third generation. George Rafferty played hooky and started sweeping hat factory floors when he was twelve, but ended up managing the last remaining hat factories in Danbury, Connecticut. Jack Lambert is second generation; His father worked for the

John B. Stetson Company his entire life.

Making a fur felt hat is not just a several-step process, as these men will explain. Although the machines referred to in the opening quote were installed to function in every step of the hat-making process, they handled only the tedious, repetitive, and heavy work. It is still the individual worker who handles and checks each raw hat body and each unblocked hat, and finishes to the supervisor's standards each straw, western, or dress hat that comes through the assembly line. Each of our hat experts will confirm this essential aspect of hat making—the quest for quality. Here are their stories.

Conversations with Hat Company Executives

Jack Lambert, Gary Rosenthal, and Robert Posey

Jack Lambert

March 4, 1998. New York City.
Jack Lambert was a vice-president for John B. Stetson, founded J. J. Hat Center, Inc., and is currently vice-president of sales for Dorfman Pacific.

DH: What would you call that color? A natural?
JL: We call it fawn or you could call it buckskin. All the colors are just names, except silver belly. Silver belly is an actual name; when they collected the beavers the name that they used to describe the skin when they turned it over or upside down (if you've ever looked at a real beaver skin) was silver belly. They never used the back because that was the worst fur. It was also the darkest and the most coarse because it would hit the ice under the streams and hit the top of their homes when they crawled under the dirt. They had the sides and then the underneath was white. It was always called the silver belly, the belly of the beaver. That's a real nostalgic term.

Here's some stuff, just to see the way they market things. Here is a flyer they would give out with the hat, giving a little story and description. This is 1949 [catalogue]. It's interesting to see. When you look at the stuff we do nowadays and you look at this, things haven't really changed significantly [points to hat]. There's the rancher. Back in those days, 3, 3½ inches were all they used. Nowadays, the most popular version of the rancher is four inches. There's your Open Road version. The Stetson Open Road, I was always told, was the number-one-selling hat ever in the history of the world. Whether Indiana Jones passed that, I doubt, just because Open Road has just been around so long. A classic hat, 5½-inch crown, 2⅞-inch brim, but then they always had variations on crowns, brims. You could buy it in regular, long, or wide ovals. One of the unfortunate things was when John B. Stetson closed up they lost all of those crown and brim blocks. A lot of that was just scrapped.

Stetson brought the rodeo back to New York in 1981. It was the only time it has been here in recent time. Historically, if you look up any of the old rodeo ideas, rodeo always ended up in Madison Square Garden in New York City, traditionally, for years and years and years, and that's where the big money was. Then, of course, as western hats lost favor, or flavor, it wound up being something that just never made it to New York

anymore, and that's the program from that [*points to rodeo program*].

Here's 1925 hat literature. A lot of this is lifted from the yearbooks. Here's another little brochure, "The Making of a Stetson Hat" in Philadelphia. They've had different variations of this book; in fact, I think we have several variations here or at home. I have a lot of these original postcards. These were all done in postcard form in the old days, especially of the general meeting—that's one of the famous ones. Everyone would come in at Christmas time, and John B. would shake their hand and give them a turkey and give them their bonuses, whatever they got. This [brochure described] the programs and policies that the company had, everything you needed to know about being a good employee. It's kind of like the employee handbook. Not many of those around that I've seen.

When I was a younger fellow, my dad, of course, worked for Stetson for forty-one years and I got involved, and I always like this history stuff. To a lot of the guys that worked there it was just like old stuff to them, and they were chucking it out, and I was always grabbing everything that my dad and his friends had, to hold onto. And then when I started going down to Philadelphia—Philadelphia was no longer a plant—I found out about Charlie K. Schaffer. Charlie started in the mail room and wound up as managing director of the company, and on the board of directors—the whole nine yards. At that time he lived in Ardmore, Pennsylvania, in a home. I used to visit him there and we would just sit there in the afternoon and just talk about old Stetson stuff. He was the last living guy that worked with John B. Stetson. When he passed away, he willed me his collection of stuff, which included all the little yearbooks the company put out. He had a set of those. He said I was the only one that had ever come and visited or ever wanted to talk about Stetson—"nobody else cared."

You've probably seen the Hubbard book, "A Little Journey." Here's "How to Use the Trademarks"; there are some of those around. This is *Coronet Magazine*.

3. The System of Hat Making

Follow the "Metal" Urge to Smartness

Winning colors at any big game this Fall are these new metal-shade felts. Left: Stetson's "Chatwood" in antique bronze...a softly furred "metal blend" felt that touches new heights of color smartness. Right: "Ballinger" in Anaconda ...with its wider brim blocked in a rolling curl. Ask to see it, too, in smart gun-metal gray.

Hard to choose between these new Stetsons isn't it? Each one is tops for its type... and tops for quality, too. That's why Stetsons are world famous. Men know that smart Stetson style will endure to the last day of wear. John B. Stetson Company, Philadelphia, New York, London, Paris. Stetsons are also made in Canada.

STETSON HATS

Stetsons, from $7.50 (unlined, from $7) to $40. Air-Light Stetsons, from $5.

How to Pick Out a Hat—*By Bob ("Best-Dressed") Benchley**

1. "Now this shape brings out the Benchley you all know...the man among men; busy, affable...dominating his circle and his affairs...the captain of his ship, master of his soul...Benchley, the successful, the envied, the admired!"

2. "Now here's a shape that brings out the old Benchley buccaneering blood... the sportsman, the dare-devil...quick to resent a slur, or to compliment a pretty woman...Buck Benchley, and will he head them off at Eagle Pass!"

3. "Now this shape emphasizes the Benchley nobody knows...scion of the banking Benchleys...cool, far-sighted...a man with a flair for figures and telephone numbers...a man of integrity...definitely a high-class guy."

4. "I like all three shapes...but can't decide...don't want a hat anyway...just... er...dropped in...*what!!!*...it's the same hat!...the Stetson 'Three-Way'...one hat with three shapes?...why, certainly, I'll take all three of it!"

5. "And look at this three-sided, Stetson-stamped box!...Why, the simon-pure, true-blue Benchley, lover of the beautiful, would carry the hat and wear the box...and by golly, as soon as I got out of sight of that hat store, I will!"

ANOTHER STETSON ORIGINAL

New Stetson design, specially constructed to look equally smart, no matter which of these three ways you choose to wear it:

1 Snap Brim **2** Brim Down All Around **3** Brim Up All Around

STETSON
"Three-Way"
$8.50

OTHER STETSONS FROM $5. STETSON HATS ARE ALSO MADE IN CANADA

* Author and Star of the Current Series of Paramount Shorts

You're not as old as I am. There used to be a magazine just like *Reader's Digest* called *Coronet*, and they had a story in there about "The Hat That Crowned the West." It was advertised and promoted on the cover as one of the stories in there. This issue happened to be given to Dave Harshaw by the mayor of Philadelphia and it's got their story in it and it's a hard-cover issue, a special issue that they did. Here's "How to Sell Hats." A lot of this was copied back and forth between "Hat Life Yearbook" and all the hat companies, Dobbs and—I do have some of that competitor stuff too. They've put out some of that stuff too. This is an old Last Drop photo, and this is an original negative that they took of the original painting way back when. I've kept that in a nice thick case. A lot of this is just articles too [*shows articles*]. Here's another old catalogue. This was 1961 [*one-page ad sheet*]. *The Stetson Century*. These are just some old photographs and negatives. These were mostly done in the 80s. There's an original of John B. that you've seen reproduced many times. Here's another version of it. Here's "America Grew Up under a Stetson"—that's when I was there. That was my regime. We did the first posters that had been done in years. They were all done in the mid-80s. More of the same pictures, I have color slides, glossies, and negatives.

DH: Please tell me about the more recent Stetson Company history.

JL: From the time the Rosenthals had the company in 1971 until it got bought out by John B. again in 1984—bought back, I should say—there was virtually no marketing done. There was some, but very little compared to the value of the name and what not.

DH: Tell me about the 1971 closing of the Stetson plant.

JL: Dave Harshaw in a huge, I guess you could call it a ceremony, stood in front of the John B. Stetson plant in Philadelphia and announced that they were closing. And that went out over the wire service as John B. Stetson going out of business, which, of course, it wasn't. What it was doing was closing that plant and opening up or licensing their name.

DH: So they sold the licensing rights to the Rosenthals and Stevens Hat Company. What was next?

JL: That stayed that way until April 1 of 1984, and at that point John B. Stetson Company, which had gotten reinvolved going back to about 1980—

There's almost two timelines you have here. You have a timeline under the Stevens Hat Company from '71 until '84, and not much was happening there except Stevens was producing hats under license; and sales, unfortunately, were going down. And I guess there was a lot of controversy about why sales were going down. Some of it was just the natural lack of enthusiasm about hats in general. Depending on who you speak to, you'll get several different answers about that. However, I believe that the John B. Company, around 1980 or so, hired an outside consultant named Allen Feinberg to do some marketing for them (so this is on your other timeline). He's the fellow that was responsible. He was a Fullbright scholar from Detroit. He married an Israeli girl. He served in the Israeli army during the '67 war—very, very intelligent, very smart, brilliant type of guy, a real marketing guru. He had been hired by Ira Guilden. Ira Guilden was the owner of the John B. Stetson Company. He owned it lock, stock, and barrel, which at the time was a holding company. And I guess between them they worked on getting the Stetson name out there more. There were several smaller things, but the first major coup happened in 1981 when Cody worked a deal to do the cologne. Cody, because they had a lot more resources than any hat company ever had, did a huge marketing research study on Stetson.

The answers or results that came back from that marketing study were that the Stetson name was recognized by virtually everyone and that the one word when they asked for a connecting word was QUALITY. So Cody immediately thought that this would be an opportunity to take a name—and, of course, Allen was able to take advantage of that whole study and use that to work with other licensing venues. He also reactivated the worldwide licensing group.

At that point Stetson had licenses with South Africa, Australia, Norway, France, Italy, Spain, England, and one more. Norcap had it in Norway, Tesse had it in Italy, Failsworth had it in England, Krems had it in France, Industrios Sombreros had it in Spain, Kubra had it in Australia, Dorian had it in South Africa, and still one more— Allen reinstated having May 1st, May Day, or thereabouts, reunions of all the licensees. They would come in from all over the world and basically give a report on the hat industry in their country and they all started doing some cross-marketing.

Allen was realizing more and more that the Stetson name could be sold in other countries, and that Americana—like Zippo lighters, and Jeep, and some of the other classic names, etc., etc.—held a prominence in the rest of the world. He got very aggressive about promoting the Stetson name. In fact, that was at the tail end of the western boom, '80 and '81, and he's the one responsible for bringing the rodeo back to New York, which gave Stetson [visibility], because it was called the world's toughest rodeo, sponsored by Stetson. It gave it a tremendous amount of publicity in a major market, which is just what it needed at the time because it got people in the cities thinking cowboy hats. That rodeo was held in the winter, December.

Quickly following thereafter, in May of '82, came the first Indiana Jones film, and Allen immediately contacted Lucas Films and worked out getting a license. Now that was after the fact, of course; the movie had come out. However, it put Stetson in a good position for movie number two, which Lucas Films already had in the works, and they knew they were going to do a whole series of these Indiana Jones movies if the first one was successful—that's all history now. It's probably one of the most successful movie groups to come out, just like *Star Wars*.

Allen started working with other groups like Zyla Wear doing glasses, so there was now an eyeglass manufacturer. One of the nice things he tried to do was that he coordinated when Stetson had a catalogue, he had some of the models wear glasses. The glasses were without lenses so there wouldn't be any reflections. And, of course, Zyla Wear was using the hats in *their* ads, and Cody was using the hats in *their* ads, and it was all coming together very nicely. Ira Guilden was getting very excited. Ira was the $100 million man because his rumored assets were $100 million. His only claim to fame was Stetson. Most of his money was from investments, and now Stetson was finally coming into the prominence that Ira had always wanted. He was very excited to have Allen doing these things. Of course, sales were starting to grow too. During that same period Allen started negotiating with Stetson.

In 1983, early '84, Allen Feinberg and Ira Guilden were negotiating with the Steven's Hat Company, which was owned by the Rosenthal family. Eventually a deal was struck on April first of '84. John B. Stetson Company became an operating company again, as opposed to a licensing company, and owned Stevens Hat Company lock, stock, and barrel. In addition to the Steven's Hat Company at that time there was the Biltmore Hat Company in Canada, which was a wholly owned subsidiary. Biltmore was actually purchased by John B. Stetson prior to the purchase of Stevens Hat Company. I believe there was a bankruptcy in Canada in 1982 and that was a direct result of a huge inventory of western bodies and western type hats and Biltmore was unable to absorb those. However, Biltmore at the time was the number-two licensee in the world, in other words, giving the second highest income to John B. Stetson Company. It was an important factor in the history of Stetson, having a Canadian operating company. Stetson decided to buy the Biltmore Hat Company. That was in '82. However, they allowed the Rosenthal family to run the company as managers for them although the Rosenthals had no ownership of the Biltmore Company.

DH: Where does Resistol fit in?

JL: Nowhere. They're competitors, two separate companies.

So now John B. Stetson owned United Fur

3. The System of Hat Making

THE GIRL IS WEARING A STETSON, TOO. IT IS CALLED PARADE. STETSON MILLINERY FASHIONS ARE PRICED FROM $6.95.

"What a pair of scene-stealers you are!"

1. The girl in the picture is kidding, of course. She'd be the first to complain if these two showed up out of focus!

They're right in step with the Easter parade—as you will be—in clothes picked with the occasion in mind. And if you think that calls for a house full of clothes—or spending a lot of money—you're wrong. It's simply a matter of choosing an outfit appropriate to the time and place.

Take these dress-up town outfits, for example...

2. For formal town wear, pick a striped brown worsted and a natural covert topcoat—they go together like Easter palms and organ music. Add color to the picture with a gay red-and-yellow-figured black tie, set off by a cream-colored shirt—and top it off with the narrow brim Stetson Vogue, in smooth Chocolate Brown.

3. Or go as the fellow at right does. Pick a neat gray worsted suit, worn with a black-and-white herringbone Shetland topcoat. Add a note of color with a dark green tie, figured in red and silver, and a crisp white shirt. Complete the metropolitan effect with a narrow brim Stetson Diplomat in the smart Sage tone.

STETSON Narrow Brim Hats — Right for Sunday morning

The name Stetson in a hat is your assurance of quality and style. Stetson hats are made only by John B. Stetson Company and its subsidiary companies—in the United States and Canada.

HAT TALK

THE GIRL IS WEARING A STETSON, TOO. IT IS CALLED ENCORE, $14.95. STETSON MILLINERY FASHIONS ARE PRICED FROM $6.95.

How to strike a perfect chord { *going to the theatre / going about your business*

The two men above are wearing hats that are perfectly in tune with the rest of their attire—and the occasion. If they swapped hats the picture would be off key.

The man hustling to a business meeting wears the brisk Stetson *Whippet*, right for well-groomed town wear. The theatregoer wears a narrow-brim Stetson *Vogue*, right for dress-up events.

For details of their outfits, see below. To bolster your hat wardrobe, see your Stetson dealer. Prices begin at $8.50.

RIGHT FOR TOWN WEAR: *The Whippet*

The perfectly proportioned *Whippet* is the most popular Stetson for town wear. In briar, it goes handsomely with a neutral tan-gray topcoat, yellow shirt, and a yellow-striped black tie. $10.

RIGHT FOR DRESS-UP: *The Vogue*

The Stetson *Vogue*, with its narrow, off-the-face brim, adds a final touch of dressiness. In flint, it looks fine with blue double-breasted suit, white shirt, checked tie, and covert cloth topcoat. $12.50.

Wear the right hat for the occasion! # STETSON HATS

More people wear Stetson Hats than any other brand. Stetson Hats are made only by John B. Stetson Company and its subsidiary companies in the United States and Canada.

Cutting, which actually cut the fur in Newark, New Jersey; Danbury Hat Company, which was the factory that actually blew the bodies; Stevens Hat Company, which was the place that finished the hats; and Biltmore, which also finished the hats. Since Stetson now owned the whole thing, there was a decision to sell all the hat bodies from Danbury to both Canada and the United States. They were all inter-company sales, so they no longer needed a body factory up in Canada; that was dismantled and any usable equipment was brought to Danbury. John B. Stetson Company took over and started running Stevens Hat Company effective April first.

Allen was promoted by Ira to be president of the whole kit and caboodle. I was vice-president of John B. Stetson at the time, and in a relatively short period of time, within about three or four months, I was given the additional duties of becoming national sales manager for Stevens or what we called the Stetson Hat Company Group. It was a different group. So I was wearing two hats. I was working for John B. Stetson, which was the parent company, and in that position was doing corporate things such as watching trademarks, working with the licensees, and helping with overall management of the different divisions along with Allen—kind of being a "gal Friday" to Allen, because I had had experience that he didn't have. So we worked as a fairly good team, and it freed him up to do other licensing.

He was getting involved in other type product categories as well as Lucas Films. At that point, in '84, the second film came out, and our sales went right through the roof; we tried to ship out as many Indiana Jones hats as we could. Stevens Hat Company at that time, even though they had been purchased by John B. Stetson Company, had not anticipated this at all, and it really hurt because we were unable to deliver hundreds and hundreds of dozens of hats that we had orders for. So there became a little bit of a strain, you might say, between the divisions of the same company, to the point where the St. Joseph division I don't think had a lot of trust for the New York division, because New York was aggressive and going forward and attempting to do things on a worldwide basis.

DH: Two different styles.

JL: Exactly, two different styles. Meanwhile sales still continued to grow. In fact, the year that I started, our sales were $17 million and a year later we had bookings of $44 million. We were on a very aggressive growth pattern. During that same time period, on and off, there were negotiations. Levi Strauss owned a company called Resistol, which was Hat Corporation of America. They had purchased it and had not done a good job with it and they were attempting to sell it. They had come to Allen in hopes that Stetson would buy them; however, our plate was pretty full at the time, and the deal was never able to be consummated. I know it got very close at times.

One of the issues, a key issue that blocked it: they have a plant down in Longview, Texas; the back of that plant had chemicals dropped in the ground for many, many years and the EPA had an "ongoing situation" there that was requiring about $100 million a year to percolate water into the ground level to get those chemicals to come back up that had been dumped in there forever. They were chemicals like carbon tetrachloride that were used in cleaning the fur. I guess these things are extremely poisonous to the environment, and that was part of the deal-breaker. Ira Guilden was excited about the prospect of owning the whole thing, but he was still a businessman at heart. I was not privy to the negotiations, but I was aware of them from second-hand knowledge. I know that those things did affect it. That was a side negotiation. When that deal did not go through, that's where AJD Company, which was a cap company in Richmond, Virginia, owned by a fellow named Irving Joel, came in. Irving Joel wound up purchasing Hat Corporation, which was Resistol and Dobbs and Knox and Cavanaugh—all these other brands.

They had always been the main competitor to Stetson historically, and there was some excitement to having a new competitor and maybe having some new blood there. However, as it worked out (and this would

53

also be considered as being a little controversial), Irving was not necessarily the best hatter. He was a good businessman. In fact, he did the ultimate business deal when he sold that company to Hat Co. or Hat Brands, because they overpaid significantly for the value of the company.

Unfortunately, Irving Joel died about six months after the deal so he didn't get to revel in the wonderful prospect, but I guess his family is still reaping the rewards. But he did the ultimate deal and sold it for way more than the value. I believe Hat Brands is still trying to recover from that deal. So that's kind of a sidebar on the competition at the time.

During late 1984 (I believe it was '84) Ira Guilden died. You can probably check that out. Unfortunately for Allen, this was his mentor, and the person who gave Allen the strength, money, ideas, support, etc., etc., etc., to do what Allen had accomplished so far.

DH: So now what happened?

JL: So now the company is owned by three people. Paul Guilden represents Ira's first marriage, Frances Gardner represents the second marriage, and Tamara Guilden is his third wife. At that time Tamara is very quiet, noninvolved on any point; however, she is still having a lot of conversations with Allen because she was still part of the family and she knew Ira's relationship with Allen, so there was a lot of trust there. However, as the year went by (I'm assuming a little bit of this now), Tamara lost a little bit of interest in keeping tabs on what was going on. Meanwhile, Paul and Frances were getting more and more anxious to get inolved. Now this was during the year 1985.

So, all of a sudden, this company that was growing tremendously seemed to be going in different directions, in my opinion. By the end of the year, a decision had been made, fairly confidentially, and unbeknownst to all of us. At the December board meeting Allen walks out—and he's fired. It took all of us by surprise. I think the company at that moment in time was totally wallowing. Nobody knew who was going to do what. We had no new direction to go. It was decided (I don't know if at that board meeting but shortly thereafter) that Frances was to be the new president of the company and Paul would be the vice-president. I think there was some question as to the amount of time Allen put in, because Allen was a workaholic. He literally would come to work at five or six in the morning. He would fall asleep at the desk at six or seven at night and still be going. He would work weekends. He was always on the job, so to speak.

Things were not too good after Allen left. By July of that year, bankruptcy was declared. It was a voluntary bankruptcy. And that ends that chapter on the company.

DH: What were some of the projects lost by this bankruptcy?

JL: Allen had been working with Hart, Schaffner and Marx to do a couple of licensings, one of which was Walter Holmes; another was Austin Reed. It opened another project, that he put me on, which was—could we possibly get the Hart, Schaffner, and Marx business to do their stores. Because 440 stores—just basing on the products that it would take to fill the shelves—would be about $2.5 million. Then if we were able to put the right product on the shelves and do two or three turns, we were talking a five-, seven-, maybe ten-million-dollar deal out of this. We worked on this project for about a year. We wound up getting the whole thing. It was a real feather in my cap. It took a lot of time, effort, and work, but it was a fun project to work on. The company declined the deal. I had to go back to Hart, Schaffner, and Marx after traveling halfway around the country—it took a year to put this thing together—and say thank you very much for giving us the deal and we don't want it.

A second thing happened during that same period in early 1986. There was another deal that we had been working on. I had met a sales contractor in Italy and I met him at the Sems show that we did in Paris. We had a booth there because we had an agent in Paris. I went over and worked in that show. We had a fellow that sold Timberland boots in Italy. He had sold 400 and then

3. THE SYSTEM OF HAT MAKING

Topper buys a hat...

By Roland Young

TOPPER: "Yes, I must say I rather like this hat snapped down in front. Gives a chap a touch of worldliness, don't you think?... Say, what's the matter with you? You act like you'd seen a ghost."
SALESMAN: ! ! ! X ? X X X ? ! ! X !

TOPPER: "Hmmmm. Like it down all around, too! Suggests a bit of dash ... a slight touch of swagger ... a sort of 'come-what-may' effect. Now, be a good fellow. Stop that nonsense and show some interest."
SALESMAN: ! ! X ? X X ! ?

TOPPER: "Well, isn't this something! Brim up all around. Here I am a respectable citizen, with that backbone-of-America look! Why, this hat can play any role! Amazing, isn't it? *Will* you stop gaping!"
SALESMAN: X ! ! ?

SALESMAN: "Jeepers, Mr. Young! You certainly gave me a start! Now that I've got my breath, I can tell you it's one hat specially designed to be worn equally well three different ways ... a hat that's bound to add a lot to a man's appearance ... and I'm not trying to be funny!"

"Three-Way" Hat Box: Handsome...triangular... specially made for the Stetson "Three-Way"... an ornament to any closet shelf...you can set it up this way.

FOR VICTORY—Buy United States Savings Bonds and Stamps

ANOTHER STETSON ORIGINAL

Stetson "Three-Way" $8.50

New Stetson design, specially constructed to look equally smart, no matter which of these three ways you choose to wear it: **1** *Snap Brim* **2** *Brim Down All Around* **3** *Brim Up All Around*

STETSON HATS ARE ALSO MADE IN CANADA

800 thousand pairs of Timberland boots in the previous two years, and now he was looking for some more Americana to sell. He wanted Stetson hats. He was not necessarily interested in first-quality hats. One of the problems we have historically in the hat industry, we have a lot of KDs or knockdowns where the hats are not absolutely perfect. As it works out, he would be willing to take all of our knockdowns. Now these hats are virtually perfect, but they are not absolutely perfect, and cowboys look at them with a magnifying glass when they first buy them. They look like crap after they've worn them for a while, but in the beginning they want them to be perfect hats. However, Europeans look at them and they just put them on as part of the image—if the price is right. So we negotiated a bit of a discount on the product and he offered—no, he actually said he wanted to purchase hats, and he gave me a schedule where he would have two containers of hats in Italy all the time; he wanted one in the water all the time, and one in the port of New York all the time, one in our warehouse, packed, all the time. He just wanted this flow to continue. He would do it all on letters of credit, so all this was paid for, so it was really a clean deal. And this deal was also turned down.

At that point in time, me being maybe not the brightest person in the whole world, but having two deals fall apart within two months, both of which were of significant value to the company and profitable to the company, the light bulb finally went on that I should stop and look at the controversy surrounding this thing and where this was going.

When the bankruptcy occurred in July of '86, they were able to get out of all the leases, out of all the contracts. Bankruptcy protection allows you to do this, with employees, such as myself. So they declared, about two or three weeks, maybe about a month after the bankruptcy, I was no longer needed with the company. They let most of the management go in most of the divisions, all the way down to line managers that were producing hats in Missouri, in an attempt "to save money.

" In my opinion it wasn't a matter of having to save money so much as just put the sales back on the sheets that we had. We had sales in house that we weren't delivering for a variety of reasons, most of which was the lack of desire of our new management to fulfill contracts that we had. So it was a very controversial time. The company floundered for about two years.

DH: How did this affect the industry?

JL: Well, when John B. Stetson Company is in bankruptcy, that hurts the whole industry. There is no one in the hat industry that had any pressure on Stetson to pay their bills or to cause a bankruptcy. The banks were cooperative. We were the largest customer of virtually every supplier, so any supplier would have said, "Hey, if you need an extra month or three months, or whatever, you got it," because they had a vested interest in seeing Stetson survive. And of course, the parts being greater than the sum in this case, the parts for all of these individual suppliers were critical for their survival. They did not want to see the company go under and the bills not get paid, and were very willing to help Stetson out. Stetson was a very good supplier and the people there were good people.

It didn't happen; the bankruptcy was declared regardless, and over that two-year period the company, and the sales, and everything else floundered. People were brought in that had no clue about the hat business. It was a very, very difficult time. Retailers started seeing no deliveries, nondeliveries, bad product. They were finding bodies out there and making hats out of them in order to save money that had moth holes in them and things like that. It was a very discouraging time for myself personally as well as any of the people that had been connected, because we were on such a high, seeing the company grow so quickly, so fast, and then to see it go down just as quickly. So it was very difficult.

Then in the fall of '88, about two years and a couple of months later, Irving Joel made his contacts or deal with Stetson to actually buy the license and he started a company called Hat Brands. Now he owned

Resistol at the time (as I said earlier, he bought it from Levi Strauss). Now he purchased the license or the rights to produce Stetson product. In that same deal, several things happened. John B. Stetson became an independent company again. They received the money from Irving. The people that had been owed money were paid off, I heard, virtually intact. I think most people got what they were owed. I don't think there was any loss, just a two-year delay while it all happened. But that all goes back to the fact that, in my opinion, it didn't ever have to happen. So there was enough money there and the assets of the company, even being purchased, were enough to cover the debts. In the same breath, Biltmore Hats of Canada, which never wanted to partake in the bankruptcy anyway, because they were solid after Stetson bought them and took their inventory off their hands, went independent again. So all in that same deal John B. Stetson became an independent company again, Biltmore became an independent company, and the license went to Hat Brands.

DH: And all the factories, all the machinery?

JL: Correct. That's part of the licensing deal. He also took over the operation of all of the factories and took them off of John B. Stetson's hands. The first thing he did, he decided to close Danbury, because he didn't need two body factories. In a very controversial move he took what was of value and brought it down to his body factory in Texas, and he took a sledge hammer to all of the other equipment up there as opposed to selling it to other companies because he felt that the less competition he had the better. The Newark fur-cutting plant stayed open for a while, but Resistol also had a fur-cutting plant in Newark. It was always in Newark because that was where the fur came into the country. It had to stay in cold storage because these furs were skins and they rotted quickly. It had to be harvested and serviced all at the port of entry. He left St. Joseph, Missouri, open as a finishing plant for Stetson. He kept his plants in Texas open to operate his Resistol and other brands there. Biltmore went off on its own. Of course, later on, Irving went on, selling the whole thing to Hicks, Muse, and that's a separate history. And they have since divided it up. They have resold it individually, I guess, to Tom Hicks, one of the owners, and changed the name to Hatco and Area Headwear, but they still only have the license for John B. Stetson. They have the license to produce the hats, and they own the Hat Corporation names which are Resistol and Dobbs.

DH: What did you do after that?

JL: I started J. J. Hat Center, Inc. with some help from my father and my wife and children. I sold the store recently to Aida O'Toole, January first last year. That was after consulting with the family; my son, at this stage of his life anyway, had no desire to get involved in the headwear business.

I've been very fortunate in my own career, my own background. I love the business.

Gary Rosenthal

December 30, 1998
Hatco Company offices, Garland, Texas

DH: Mr. Rosenthal, could you give us a brief summary of the history of the Stevens Hat Company?

GR: The Stevens Hat Company originated in 1917 in St. Joseph, Missouri. At that time it was not known as the Steven's Hat Company, but the St. Joseph Hat and Cap Company. It was a regional cap company. My grandfather was a cap maker. His partner, whose family name is Pitluck, was also a cap maker. And the oldest uncle, who was by then about twenty-one, started the company in 1917 in a very small regional way.

It grew and survived through the depression years. In the early or middle thirties they wanted to go into more of a national scope in the central part of the country. That was when they changed the name of the

HAT TALK

THE SATURDAY EVENING POST   April 13, 1935

STETSON

It is a fugitive thing, this element called Style. But it can mean so much to a man...and to a creator of hats. To guess wrong may be not only futile but fatal. *Stetson has removed the last faint shadow of doubt...first for the hats and, second, for the men who wear them.*

REGULAR-WEIGHT STETSONS ARE $6.50 (*unlined* $6), $8, $10 AND UP. The Playboy and the Bantam (*air-light Stetsons*) are $5

STETSON
JOHN B. STETSON COMPANY
PHILADELPHIA

The mark of the world's most famous hat

company to the Stevens Hat Company. They operated as a manufacturer and jobber of men's headwear, both caps and hats, for many years out of St. Joseph, Missouri. They had salesmen covering a good part of the country from the Midwest, South, and West—Texas, California, and in between.

I started working at the factory when I was about fourteen, working in the factory when school was out.

DH: Did you have specific jobs?

GR: Well, in those days, I guess I started in the shipping department, sweeping, because that was something unskilled I could do at the time. When I was about sixteen, or maybe younger than that, I was put in the hat factory. I remember I was too short to reach the levers on the machine, so I had to stand on a Coke box (they tell me). Anyway, I grew up doing that every summer.

In those days hat making was a lot of hand-finishing; you would take the sandpaper and the grease bags, and do it all by hand. Even though we had machines, we still touched them up and worked them by hand. We could do maybe four or five dozen hats a day by hand. And it was a lot of work in the hot summer.

I went to college in 1950 and came back from the Navy in '56, and went to work full time. By 1960, our company was ready to expand. We started acquiring other regional hat companies—not major, but middle-size companies. We acquired a company in Minneapolis called Trimble Hat Company, in Chicago, Portis Hat Company. Portis was a good label and they were right at the same price point as Stevens was—what we call middle range, underneath Stetson, underneath Dobbs, and so forth. Portis was a good shot for us because it doubled our size overnight.

By the late '60s we were in touch with the owners of Stetson. In 1965 control of John B. Stetson was purchased by New York financiers. They were investment people (Ira Guilden and Philip Roth) who wanted to get out of some of the manufacturing processes. And our company happened to have body factories in Danbury and Bethel, Connecticut. We made arrangements to open the Mallory hat factory in Danbury, which was sitting idle. Stetson had bought Mallory in about 1960. It was a large plant, but inactive. So they shut down the Philadelphia body-making facility and we became partners with Stetson in the body factory. It was called Danbury Hat Company. We (our people) were the managers and financially we were partners with the John B. Stetson Company.

In 1970 John B. Stetson was looking to really get out of being an operational company and we made arrangements to buy the company. We bought all the assets of the company except the label. We took forty truckloads of equipment and product out of the Philadelphia plant, and moved it to our factory in St. Joseph, Missouri. It was quite an undertaking. We took over their sales force. We were the Stetson Company in the United States. We operated as the Stetson Hat Company, and that was the visible company for the sale and manufacture of Stetson hats in the United States. At that time we were not selling Stetson product outside the United States, because they had at that time licensees in other countries—South Africa, Germany, Italy.

DH: Was Biltmore part of this?

GR: No, that's another story. There was a Stetson hat factory in Canada which John B. Stetson owned, but they phased out before we got there. Our company bought the Biltmore Company in 1982 right after the *Urban Cowboy* crash. We bought it outright and operated it. In fact, my son, John Rosenthal, who is the fourth generation in our business, went up there and ran the company for a couple of years.

You're well aware of the *Urban Cowboy* boom in 1978, '79, '80, and '81. In November '81 it fell flat. What it really did was go back to normalcy, because the *Urban Cowboy* was a completely abnormal situation. Wonderful as it was for the sales of hats, a lot of people got hurt because they over-extended themselves. We fortunately didn't invest in what we call mortar and bricks. We didn't build factories and so forth. We worked extra shifts and all the things you did to try to deliver, but a lot of people got caught and cancellations were horrible.

DH: By 1982 you have everything; you're manufacturing Stetson, you've got Biltmore, so you're the only manufacturer in the country, besides Resistol.

GR: No, that's not true. There were then and still are other hat companies.

I was president of the company. My father, Ben Rosenthal, who was chairman, passed away in 1975.

In 1984 we agreed to sell our private company, Stevens Hat Manufacturing Company, back to John B. Stetson, who at that time had some new management and they decided they wanted to be an operational company again.

DH: When you sold to Stetson, you were still running the plant in St. Joe?

GR: I continued as president of the company until 1986. Between 1984 and 1986 the company became overextended and took Chapter 11 in June of 1986. My contract was revoked in September of '86.

After about three months of walking around the house, I was getting itchy. One of my good personal friends, Irving Joel, owned AJD Cap in Richmond and had bought Miller Brothers Hat Company in '84 and bought Resistol in '85. He said, "Gary why don't you come with me?" So I got back in the hat business with him. I was with him in an executive capacity, doing customer service work. I knew a lot of people. I was in the business. I still lived in St. Joe. I didn't move down here until '94, when the next regime came on board.

DH: When did the company change ownership?

GR: Hicks, Muse bought the Resistol Company from Irving Joel in October of '92 and Hicks, Muse set up their own management people. The headquarters were going to be in Garland, Texas.

I was asked if I would like to move to Dallas and take over the dress hat division. Which I did.

Hicks, Muse owns the division called Arena Brands. Arena Brands, which is headquartered here, owns Hatco, Montana Silversmith, Imperial Cap Company in Denver, and Lucchese Boot Company of El Paso. John Tillitson is president of Arena Brands and Thom Harris is president of Hatco.

DH: So your company is doing well, I hope.

GR: Yes, we're pleased to be able to come along pretty well. The hat industry, of course, is very closely tied with the western industry, and we continue to make western hats and dress hats.

We still operate the St. Joseph factory. It makes the Stetson felts. The Garland factory makes the Resistol felts, and makes all of the straws for Stetson and Resistol (in this building right over here). We have the two factories going with the body factory in Longview, Texas, and the fur-cutting factory in Newark, New Jersey. That's our production facilities.

DH: People who see the hat exhibit are always amazed at how many steps it takes to make a felt hat. From all we've heard, the hat business is a tricky one.

GR: Yes. It's probably the most unique. The technology is the same as it was fifty years ago or seventy years ago. Hat making is still the same. It still comes from the pelts of rabbits and beavers, shaved off and processed, the hood being shrunk down to size. Because, as you know, there's no adhesive; it's just locked together with the fibers of the fur. It's a unique process.

Robert Posey

December 30, 1998, Dallas, Texas
Bob Posey was with Resistol for more than thirty years and is now product development manager for Hatco.

DH: We missed interviewing Ken Jewell.

BP: I have a special fondness for him. I'm just going to touch on something. In modern days, Ken probably knew the carriage hat trade better than anybody. I was lucky enough, and I say lucky, that I worked, and John Milano was my mentor for twenty-some years. And I worked with three guys mainly. One was Ken Jewell, [there was] John Milano, and another guy named Bernie Venner. Have you heard of him?

DH: No.

BP: He pioneered the West for Harry Rolnick—Harry Rolnick, who founded this company. He was a real character. There are so many funny stories about him, but he wasn't just a character. He was impressive.

Harry Rolnick was someone you would have loved to have known. This was a real gentleman—a real class act. Rose Rolnick is still alive.

DH: We found from doing the hat exhibit that everyone has a hat story. Many people, even though they don't wear their hats, have closets full of them.

BP: Pride of ownership. Gary and I would be on an elevator in New York or somewhere, fairly recent history, and you get on the elevator and people would go—I didn't know people still wore hats.

I tell you what has changed—which brings up a good point. In ads today, there's a good chance, and I don't know if this is positive toward what you want to do, but anyway— For a long time, in the late '60s and early '70s, I guess, if hats were used in ads, they were on top of a buffoon. In fact, there was a comedian, Stanley Myron Handelman, who wore a cap. And one time he came to Dallas to entertain, and the president of the company at that time said grab a few hats and take them over to him, because he wears caps. And I said I would not. And he said, "Why don't you want to?" And I said, "Because he wears them as a prop to look like a dufuss. In other words, a negative image." That wasn't well received, but you understand my point? In a lot of times in that era, and I don't mean it's not done today, hats were for comic or silly effect. As a matter of fact, in a lot of the clip art that you see, the Deco type contains this.

Have you touched on the Jewish community in Brooklyn?

DH: No, not yet. We have not gone beyond regular formal wear—western and dress hats.

BP: It's very important in the industry.

DH: And the Mennonites.

BP: And in many cases they wear them a little higher up on the head, don't they? But what I mean: somebody might think, boy, that brim's awfully big, but when the hat is worn higher up, the bigger brim is proportionate. In fact, I was in retail and dress hats when people wore the bigger brims. Then brims went narrower and we increased the size of the hat for the people, and brought them down farther, so that little brims didn't look so dopey up top where they used to wear the big brims.

DH: Have you come across any of the historical records of the company?

BP: We had a new advertising guy. What this company was is the amalgamation of many, many, many best brands throughout the hat history in the United States. And there was an enormous amount of old artwork and dyes. And one day I went into the old file cabinet (you already know where this story is going). You know how a drawer crammed full is heavy, and you have to pull the little lever. I yanked it, and almost fell down because I was expecting to pull this heavy thing. And then I immediately thought, oh crimanies, they've taken this and put it in one of those big storage boxes in warehouse seven. That's where they put this stuff. It's summer and it's 120 degrees up in that loft where they keep this stuff, and I thought, oh I've got to go up there and find this stuff. I go and ask the guy, is it up in warehouse seven? And the guy says, nah, I threw all that stuff out. It happened fairly recently when they moved some of the stuff over there. We lost an enormous amount of records. There's a penchant for "old is bad."

DH: John Milano told us that he evolved the whole synthetic straw hat process for Resistol. Is that correct?

BP: Shantung. Yes. He devoted an enormous amount of time to developing the Shantung straw.

BP: The hat salesman at that time (1940s) was second only in prestige to the suit salesman.

A lot of the salesmen had a packer who would go

This Indenture Witnesseth, THAT _Joseph Gasz Born December 18th 1867_ by and with the consent of _Christine Gasz his mother_ hath put himself, and by these presents doth voluntarily and of his own free will and accord, put himself Apprentice to JOHN B. STETSON, his heirs or assigns, to learn the art, trade and mystery of _Felt hat finishing_ and after the manner of an Apprentice to serve the said JOHN B. STETSON, his heirs or assigns, for and during, and to the full end and term of his Apprenticeship, which will be the _Thirteenth day of June 1887_ next ensuing.

The said Master reserving the right to terminate this agreement, if said Apprentice shall refuse to obey his proper commands, or shall be found physically unable to attend to his work. During all which time the said Apprentice doth covenant and promise, that he will serve his Master faithfully, keep his secrets and obey his lawful commands; that he will do him no damage himself, nor see it done by others without giving him notice thereof; that he will not waste his goods, nor lend them unlawfully; that he will not contract matrimony within the said term; that he will not play at cards, dice, or any other unlawful game, whereby his Master may be injured; that he will neither buy nor sell, with his own goods or the goods of others, without license from his Master; and that he will not absent himself day nor night from his Master's service without his leave, nor haunt ale houses, taverns, or play houses, but in all things behave himself as a faithful Apprentice ought to do during the said term. He shall conform to and abide by all rules and regulations now in force, and hereafter adopted by his Master, for the government of his Apprentices. And the said Master on his part doth covenant and promise, that he will use the utmost of his endeavors to teach, or cause to be taught or instructed, the said Apprentice in the art, trade, or mystery of _Felt hat finishing_ and he shall receive as compensation, when working, two ($2.00) dollars per week.

It appearing upon satisfactory proof, that said minor has been properly educated in reading, writing, and arithmetic, so as to render further schooling unnecessary.

And for the true performance of all and singular the covenants and agreements aforesaid, the said parties bind themselves each unto the other firmly by these presents.

In Witness Whereof, the said parties have interchangeably set their hands and seals hereunto. Dated the _Second_ day of _July_ in the year of our Lord one thousand eight hundred and eighty _five_.

Sealed and delivered in the presence of

Joseph Hood
Robert Smith

John B Stetson
Cristina Gas
Joseph Gasz

with them. They would travel by train with a steamer trunk full of hats. The hat departments were enormous. They would run the whole side walls of stores. And as the salesman would meet in the hotel with the account, the packers would take the hats up and set up the room. Then the various accounts would come to the hotel room, as opposed to [the salesman] going into a store and throwing the hats on top of something. Today it's not the same.

In those days all the companies prided themselves on the longevity of salesmen. They didn't want turnover and most of them didn't have it. They had guys working with thirty, forty years of tenure. This guy Bernie Venner, when I went with him traveling, he had sold the grandfather, and then the father, and now he was selling the son.

4

Everyman and His Bowler

"Appearance may be sacrificed for comfort, or conventionality purposely defined, then the *kind* of hat is varied. Individuals sometimes cling to the times and traditions of their youth; then the *style* will be more or less out of date. A desire for smartness has often led to exaggeration while utterly bad taste is accountable for many peculiarities."—*The Hatter's Gazette*, December 1900

The bowler was worn by everyman: all classes, all ranks, and all occupations. Fred Robinson Miller devotes an entire book, *The Man in the Bowler Hat: Its History and Iconography*, to a detailed look at why and with whom the bowler was so popular. His description seems to capture it perfectly:

> Urban crowds in the decades before and after the turn of the century were a sea of bowler hats. Toppers, boaters, and caps abounded as well, but the bowler crossed more class lines. Some had low crowns and a wider brim, while some had very high crowns; most had the curled brims increasingly fashionable in the latter decades; some were fawn-colored or brown or gray—and they were everywhere. In London they were worn by men doing road repairs, newshawkers, milkmen, knife grinders, rabbit sellers, and Sherbet and Water vendors—all manner of working folk who seemed to wear their bowlers as badges of the city street. Shabby workers sitting on benches outside pubs, pints in hand, set their bowlers beside them like pets. The men buying from vendors wore bowlers, men in shoddy black suits with tight shoulders and baggy pants, the types that Chaplin remembered when he contrived his costume. At times these men are difficult to distinguish from the workers and vendors; buyers and sellers blend together, as if intentionally marking out a new class or as if eager to blur the idea of class in a democracy of the street. More fashionable men, with stiffer and cleaner collars and a better cut of clothes (larger coats, narrower trousers), mingle with the others, or more likely with their top-hatter ilk near the banks of the City, or in carriages (later four-wheeled gigs), or pose in vari-

o u s p u b l i c ceremonies. And, of course, bowler-hatted cab and open omnibus drivers guide clusters of bowler-hatted middle-class men through the thronged streets. At political and labor rallies, in England and America, bowlers bob on the heads of laborers in their Sunday best as if they were crowd hats, passed out for purposes of solidarity.[1]

As Miller so eloquently expresses, the bowler hat crossed more class lines than the upper-crust toppers, the casual fedora, or the sporty straw. The bowler was worn with the dressier lounge suits that had become increasingly popular since their introduction in the 1850s.[2] They were also worn at work. *The Gentlemen's Tailor* in 1911 called the bowler "the next most dressy style of hat" to the topper.[3] From their inception in 1850 to their decline in the 1920s, bowlers were worn short and tall.

The bowler's heyday was from 1890 to around 1910. In its first catalogue of 1876 Montgomery Ward promoted five to ten styles of "derbys" (as the bowler was called in America). Called "Gents' Stiff Wool and Fur Hats," they were described as "Our finest and best Derby Hat . . . made from carefully selected stock. The workmanship and trimmings are strictly first-class."[4] Despite this generous description, the bowler had always been cheaper to make and more comfortable to wear than the top hat.

One of the famous (and now sadly closed) British hat companies, Christy Ltd. of Stockport, supplied not only their own sales force, but also finished hats with different hatters' labels for other famous independent hat-makers.[5] The variety in shape and nuance was evident in Christy's 1899 catalogue, in which twenty-one styles were pictured. The 1911 catalogue offered twelve styles, while the 1916 catalogue offered only four because of the shortage of shellac.[6] One other indicator of the bowler's popularity was its placement at the beginning of the catalogue, immediately following the silk top hats. By 1920 the Montgomery Ward catalogue pictured only one derby-type style, now called "A neat

H. R. H. the Prince of Wales tips his bowler.

Dakota Style," and placed it on a page with an Open-Road style hat, army hats, fedoras with telescoped crowns (porkpie hats), and several poplins with open, creased, and telescoped crowns.[7] Evidently derbys were more saleable in the United States; the Stetson catalogues included in the Appendix show fourteen variations for 1913, seven for 1914, and a listing of six for 1915, while the 1922 catalogue pictures eight. The Stetson catalogues show only minor variation in size and contouring of the bowlers, in contrast to the Taylor catalogue, which had more variety. As time went on, bowlers became increasingly standardized and uniform.

Another permutation of the original derby was the outsized version worn in the West. Chas. P. Shipley pictures in his 1935 catalogue what looks like an over-sized

OUR FUR STIFF HAT FIFER.

6 inches Deep, 2¼ Brim.

Quantity.		Price.
......Dozen No. 140,	Men's Black Fifer	$21.00
......Dozen No. 141,	Men's Seal-Brown Fifer	21.00
......Dozen No. 142,	Men's Pearl Fifer	21.00
......Dozen No. 143,	Men's Side Nutria Fifer	21.00

OUR FUR STIFF HAT COMRADE.

6 inches Deep, 2⅜ Brim.

Quantity.		Price.
......Dozen No. 144,	Men's Black Comrade	$18.00
......Dozen No. 145,	Men's Pearl Comrade	18.00
......Dozen No. 146,	Men's Seal-Brown Comrade	18.00

MEN'S FUR COLUMBIA.

5¾ x 2⅜.

MEN'S Fur Columbia. We have this Hat in four colors; the quality is superb for the price; shape one of the most conservative styles in our Stiff Hat line. Merchants can make no mistake in giving us big orders. Our prices are as low as any reputable manufacturer can make them.

Quantity.		Price.
......Doz. No. 151,	Men's Bronze Columbia Stiff Fur Hat	$18.00
......Doz. No. 152,	Men's Black Columbia Stiff Fur Hat	18.00
......Doz. No. 153,	Men's Brown Columbia Stiff Fur Hat	18.00
......Doz. No. 154,	Men's Pearl Columbia Stiff Fur Hat	18.00

MEN'S PENSACOLA.

6 inch x 2⅜.

OUR Men's Fur Stiff Pensacola, with wide band, handsomely lined and extra fine quality, is a great selling Hat. This is a medium full-shaped Hat, one in which merchants will take no risks by ordering in quantities. Every dollar's worth of goods quoted in this Price List is a flyer. We want your trade, and are determined to make the best storekeepers in the land come and see us, or favor us with an order.

Quantity.		Price.
......Dozen No. 155,	Men's Black Pensacola	$21.00
......Dozen No. 156,	Men's Seal-Brown Pensacola	21.00
......Dozen No. 157,	Men's Pearl Pensacola	21.00

SHREWD MERCHANT PONDER On Our Prices.

MEN'S FUR STIFF DUNLAP.

THE Dunlap is the Hat for city trade, and will have an unprecedented run for the Spring of 1889. The style is simply perfect for a staple Stiff Fur Hat; could make no improvement on the shape, and the quality is the best for the money.

Quantity.		Price.
......Dozen No. 147,	Men's Black Dunlap	$24.00
......Dozen No. 148,	Men's Brown Dunlap	24.00
......Dozen No. 149,	Men's Maple Dunlap	24.00
......Dozen No. 150,	Men's Pearl Dunlap	24.00

When writing us be sure to state your name plainly, also Town, County and State. Storekeepers sometimes forget this, and we are unable to communicate with them; then they wonder why we do not give their order attention.

MEN'S WOOL SAXONY SAVANNAH.

5¼ x 2⅜.

THE Savannah is a fine finished Saxony Stiff Hat; will outlast a cheap fur and make a handsome appearing Hat; will give perfect satisfaction. Twenty-four Line Band. Richly lined.

Quantity.		Price.
......Dozen No. 158,	Men's Tobacco-Brown Savannah	$12.00
......Dozen No. 159,	Men's Black Savannah	12.00

MEN'S FUR JEFFERSON.

6½ x 2½.

BUY this handsomely-lined Fur Stiff Hat. No merchant's Hat stock will be complete without it. The style is correct in every particular, and price three dollars less than any Hat jobber or middleman can sell them. Remember, we are no job-lot house; we do not handle boots and shoes, collars and shirt studs and watches, but we are dealers in Hats and Caps, with a big H and C.

Quantity.		Price.
......Dozen No. 160,	Men's Coffee-Brown Jefferson	$21.00
......Dozen No. 161,	Men's Black Jefferson	21.00
......Dozen No. 162,	Men's Smoked Pearl Jefferson	21.00

Pages from the Taylor Bros. 1889 spring catalogue clearly illustrate the variety in shape and brim-curling that the bowler could accommodate.

*Cambridge style bowler.
Courtesy Stockport Heritage Museum*

John McMicking holding two Cambridge style bowlers, both of which he fabricated.

Cambridge derby, called the "John B. Stetson Malta," with a 6-inch crown, and a 3½-inch brim in tan or brown.[8] The Denver Dry Goods Company catalogue for 1941–42 shows a similar hat with an oversized crown of 6¼ inches and a high-roll brim of 6½ inches. The catalogue boasts, "This hat has a lot of snap and verve."[9] These hats are seen in western films on merchants and Indians or character actors.

Although derbys/bowlers continued to be worn by the upper classes as their informal-formal hat well past the 1920s (the topper being reserved for ceremony), the middle classes had switched to the fedora, the cap, and the boater. One outstanding example was Winston Churchill. While other gentlemen of his station were wearing their Homburgs, Churchill continued to wear his Cambridge-style square-crowned bowler well into the 1940s; by then it had become his signature hat.

What was the bowler's origin? The best source (and most often quoted) is a book called *Mr. Lock of St. James's Street,* written by Frank Whitbourn in 1971 for the honorable hatters of Lock and Co. of London. He credits his information to research done by Air Vice-Marshal Geoffrey Bowler, for whose family the bowler hat continues to be named.[10]

Hat maker John McMicking says that in all of hat history there are very few definite dates. Two of them are 1850, Lock's creation of the bowler, and 1865, Lock's creation of a squared-crowned bowler for the Duke of Cambridge.[11] In those days it was the practice to name the hats after the gentlemen for whom they were designed. Originally the bowler was called a Coke. It was listed in Lock's sales book, "First one sold for twelve shillings to William Coke of Norfolk for whom it was made." The second such hat was sold to a Mr. Lawley, at which point the style was officially designated a "coke."[12]

In 1850 William Coke, nephew of the Earl of Leicester of Norfolk approached the Lock brothers in their St. James establishment. Coke wanted a hat that would protect his gamekeepers from being beaned on the noggin when racing after poachers on his country grounds. He had been providing his men a round hat called a Thanet, which kept getting caught in the low branches of trees and offered very little protection. He wanted the hardness of a top hat without its height, and also a curved surface that would more easily deflect oncoming obstacles. The solution, he told the Locks, was a close-fitting, hard, rounded hat—so the Lock brothers came up with one.

Evidently their grandfather had already invented a close-fitting riding-hat in the 1780s. The Locks got their unfinished hat bodies from William and Thomas Bowler (originally from Stockport, England—a center of hat-making), whose shop was across the River Thames in Southwark. They all consulted. William made a prototype. The actual process of felting the raw hat body was extremely important. The correct amount of fur had to be used and shellac had to be added to give the hat its needed extra strength. The resulting hat was called a bowler on the south side of the river where the hat body was made, and a coke on the north side where the hat was finished.

Because Coke wanted the hat to be hard, shellac was the key ingredient. The most famous part of this tale was described by historian Frank Whitbourn: "He put it on the floor and trod on it. The hat yielded not so much as a quarter size. It remained round, domed, undented."[13] No wonder it was dubbed the "iron hat." It was a little hard on the brow, but with a conformateur to get an accurate head shape, the coke or bowler, depending on which side of the river you chanced to live, could be fitted perfectly to your head.[14] Hat maker John McMicking considers the story of standing on the hat apocryphal. In his numerous experiments, he has found that the only hats really able to bear a person's weight are those made from shellacked layered calico and cork.

The hat's American name, derby, was adopted when the Earl of Derby wore a bowler at the Derby races. (Americans pronounce it "dur-bee" and the English say "dar-bee.") Only two of the original names have stuck. In America and American catalogues, the hat is called a derby, while in Britain and British catalogues it is called a bowler. In the trade the coke-bowler-derby is described as "a hard fur felt" which comes in light, medium and extra firm weights.[15] Americans preferred the lighter weights. When shellac was scarce during the two world

Tilt the hat and you have style.

Low-crown bowlers.

John McMicking is holding a top hat in his left hand and a Cambridge bowler in his right.

The gentleman in this picture and those on the preceding page are probably not wearing billycocks, but their rakishly tilted derbys do give them panache.

wars, hats were softer. These softer hats are the ones more commonly found in antique markets, and are still produced for costume and personal adornment by a few of the remaining hat companies, often of wool rather than fur felt.

Several other confusions surround the bowler. It is not a billycock, which is a variety of an eighteenth-century cocked hat that had been adopted by a gang of upper-class gentlemen who were out to make trouble. Their "bully" behavior was corrupted to "billy" and then to "billycock."

Another round, hardened hat, worn underground by Cornish miners, was made in Redruth by a local hat maker named William Cock. This cottage industry supplied hats for local use only. These were referred to as

The Gentlemen's Tailor, Janury 1910

Billy-cocks, after their maker.[16]

The final confusion is between the squared-off Cambridge style and the shorter top hat. The top hat is made of silk plush or silk fabric (the collapsible opera hat) while the Cambridge is made of wool or fur felt and has decidedly rounded top corners. While size may be approximately the same, construction materials and usage are quite different. In their 1900 catalogue Wards describes a Cambridge (although not calling it that; it is merely in the category of "Men's Derby Hats") as "Made with 5-inch flat top crown, 1 3/4-inch half-set brim. An exact copy of the Roloff Full Block, and different from all other shapes. They come in black only. Each . . . 3.00."[17]

It is important to remember that these hats (all hats) were worn all the time as an article of clothing, not just as an accessory. Even though the gentlemen in the photos on this page are formally posed for their studio portraits, they are dressed in the clothes that they normally wear. Hats were functional; they were worn until they were thrown or given away. Some hats were referred to as "my puttin' away hat," which meant that after the owner died, the hat was passed on to another male relative.[18] Most good hats, especially toppers, were passed on to relatives because in those times clothing was scarce and more expensive than it is today and head-gear of various kinds was a much more important aspect of the man's dress code.

One distinct use of the bowler has been in South America. The Andean Cholas, the native women from Ecuador to Chile, wear hats based upon the round-top bowler hat, and have done so since the 1920s. Perhaps the British workers who built the railroads introduced them, but these hats now signify wealth, position, and commerce according to the local custom. Made locally, they come in many colors.

Actor/director Walter Rhodes says that the contemporary impression a bowler "produces is a silhouette both jaunty and business-like." Rhodes continues:

The versatile bowler hat has been as appealing over

time to mimes, clowns, hucksters, card sharps, dancers, musicians, and artists, as it has to bankers, lawyers, and politicians. Wearing one is a dapper statement promising entertainment and professionalism of the most stylish kind. For example, can you imagine Bob Fosse's snappy jazz choreography or Fred Astaire's elegant tap routine minus the bowler hat? You cannot. Would you trust a lawyer or a judge in a bowler? Outside the courtroom you might. The classic hat is reflective of their competence, confidence, and ability to enthrall a jury.

"I acquired a vintage, English-made bowler for my fourteen-year-old son, who is an accomplished tap dancer and juggler. The times he wears it are not casually chosen. It has been an attention-getter and audience-pleaser whether he is selling toys at a street festival, demonstrating the cup and balls in a magic shop, performing in musicals, or playing lead guitar in his recently formed punk rock band. The bowler. King of the hat world![19]

Andean women wearing bowlers.

*Costumed performers posing
with men dressed for work.*

COVENTRY BLUES .... THE NEWEST AND MOST IMPORTANT COLORS IN MEN'S HEADWEAR .... FOR SPRING AND FALL .... INSPIRED BY THE FAMOUS COVENTRY BLUE .... A COLOR THAT WAS PROMINENT IN GREAT BRITAIN IN THE 12th CENTURY .... RECAPTURED BY HODSHON, BERG, INC., FIFTH AVENUE, NEW YORK .... MAKERS OF FLANUL FELT HATS .... HODSHON HATS .... BERG HATS .... SUNFAST HATS AND BERG CREST HATS .... FLANUL FELT HATS ARE FOR SALE AT B. ALTMAN & CO., NEW YORK .... AND OTHER EXCLUSIVE SHOPS THROUGHOUT THE COUNTRY .... $7.50 to $20.

5

How the Fedora Got Its "Snap"

> "A citizen of Yonkers, New York, Mr. John T. Waring, had made such improvements upon the old style wool hats of that time as to commend them greatly to popular favor. After consultation with his brother, he took his sample hat to New York and the result was an order at once for fifty dozen at a large advance on the price of hats of the old fashion and the final result, after years of successful labor and judicious improvement, was the erection of the great hat manufactory of the Waring Manufacturing Company, at Yonkers, New York."[1] —*A History of American Manufacturers, 1608 to 1860*

The soft felt hat, sometimes called the fedora, the crusher, or the Trilby, is making a comeback—or was it ever gone? There have always been soft felt hats, often worn by peasants, hand-shaped and worn for protection. These same soft felts were catapulted into the fashionably stylish category when in 1851 the Hungarian patriot, Lajos Kossuth, wore one while touring the United States and England at a time when the stiff topper was predominant. But Kossuth was certainly not the first to wear a felt hat of shaped rounded crown and wide felt brim.

The Kossuth hat's charismatic aesthetic coincided with the evolving romantic art and literature movements. It received another boost when American theater-goers saw the French writer Victorien Sardou's play *Fédora* (1881–1882), and the soft felt took that name. In 1885 the hat got its English name from another stage production, *Trilby*, by George du Maurier. The now widely popular hat had a soft felt crown that could easily be creased lengthwise, while the brim could be flanged up or down or both, at will, by the wearer instead of the hatter, giving the individual more control over his appearance.

The soft felt is credited as stimulating the growth of the hatting industry in Orange, New Jersey. Historian David Bensman, in his book *The Practice of Solidarity: American Hat Finishers in the Nineteenth Century,* states: "In Orange, which was growing rapidly because of the *new soft hat craze* [italics added], young Frederick secured a position as journeyman in a small

Opposite: Snap-brim Fedoras, ca. 1930.

An assortment of soft felt hats, some—or all—of which may be "crushers."

hat shop...."[2] This reference dates to approximately 1856, supporting the notion that the popularity of the soft felt was inspired by Lajos Kossuth.

The "crusher" is a variation on a theme—a soft wool or fur felt. An extra-light felt with a soft leather or grosgrain sweatband, it could easily be folded or "crushed" for travel, much like the finely woven Panama straw hats. The 1897 Sears, Roebuck & Company catalogue describes their crushers as having "flexible sweatbands, heavy satin lining, [and they] can be creased or not as desired." A second type of traveling hat, called a French Pocket Hat, could fold to fit in the wearer's pocket. The catalogue described it as "made from finest French fur felt, with satin lining and ribbed silk sweatband."[3] These folding, crushable hats are still produced, and are currently a specialty of the Italian Borsalino Hat Company and the English Herbert Johnson Hatters.[4]

The advantage of a soft hat over a stiff one is, of course, malleability; no conformateur is needed. The wearer can shape his hat to his own personal requirements. The basic hat remained relatively constant during the twentieth century—crowns varied little more than a couple of inches (approximately four to six), as did brims (two to four), depending on fashion. But within these minor increases and decreases, the wearer had a myriad of other choices. He could sculpt, crease, flange, or bash to his heart's content. He could find colors ranging from Borsalino pale turquoise to hundreds of shades of brown and gray. Bands were wide or narrow; they sported feathers, medals, or flat bows. In 1925 alone,

40   TAYLOR BROS. & CO., CHICAGO, PRICE LIST.

MEN'S NOBBY FUR CRUSHER DICK.

4 inch x 2⅜.

WE warrant every Hat to be perfect; we guarantee to please you in style, price and quality, and give you ten days time after receipt of goods to find out if they are as we represent; if not, return at our expense. We do not sell less than a half-dozen of any one kind.

Quantity.	Price.
......Dozen No. 194, Men's Tobacco-Brown Dick..............	$7.50
......Dozen No. 195, Men's Blue Dick.........................	7.50
......Dozen No. 196, Men's London Fog Dick..................	7 50
......Dozen No. 197, Men's Pearl Dick.......................	7.50

MEN'S WOOL CRUSHER VETO.

4 inch x 2⅜.
A nobby feather-weight, great seller.

Quantity.	Price.
......Dozen No. 198, Men's Tobacco-Brown Veto..............	$6.00
......Dozen No. 199, Men's Butternut Veto...................	6.00

While it is impossible for us to illustrate but a small portion of our stock of Hats, Caps and Straw Goods, we can assure all merchants that the ones we do quote are the choice selection out of our stock, and we will warrant the prices the lowest.

TAYLOR BROS. & CO., CHICAGO, PRICE LIST.   41

ABSOLUTELY
THE BEST
CRUSHER

In the Market for the Money.

MEN'S CRUSHER CHICAGO.

THIS is a full-shaped Hat, 5½ x 3 Brim. Look at the price we name, and order one dozen each. Remember, any Hat that does not please you can be returned at our expense. Do you take any risks in ordering goods of us? We want your trade and hope prices will bring it.

Quantity.	Price.
.....Dozen No. 200, Men's Coffee-Brown Chicago Crusher	$6.00
.....Dozen No. 201, Men's London Fog Chicago Crusher......	6.00
.....Dozen No. 202, Men's Back Nutria Chicago Crusher.........	6.00
.....Dozen No. 203, Men's Calfskin Chicago Crusher...........	6.00
.....Dozen No. 204, Men's Pearl Chicago Crusher.............	6.00
.....Dozen No. 205, Men's Blue Chicago Crusher.............	6.00

the Knox and Dunlap Company produced over nine thousand combinations of styles, colors, and sizes of men's dress hats.[5] The photographs in this chapter illustrate how the wearer customized his hat to suit himself.

Crown heights went up and down, while a variety of sizes and shapes were worn. In a picture taken in 1905, my grandfather sports a short-crowned soft felt, worn straight and flat. During the 1960s, the fedora brims were their narrowest, and vibrant colors matched citrus-colored fashions. The longer plush fur felt in pale green with its narrow brim and matching fur-felt hat band (shown at

1960s chartreuse, long-napped fedora

Gentleman wearing a soft felt "crusher."

Young man holding a soft felt fedora, ca. 1890. Like the three gentleman in the photograph at the left, he seems to have randomly punched his hat, giving it an improvised look.

These hats all fall into the general category of fedora. Hats at center and right appear to have rolled brims.

5. How the Fedora Got Its "Snap"

My father-in-law, Ben Hudson, wears his fedora at a rakish angle, while my father (top right) wears his hat centered and a little high on his forehead.

"Soft felt hats with no brim roll and with the telescoped crown were called a 'pork pie.' This is technically a fedora, but has acquired a more specific name to indicate the precise style of the hat."
—John McMicking, hat maker
The pork pie shown at the right is worn by my grandfather in 1905.

These unknown workers wear soft felts with their overalls and jackets.

An unknown gentleman balances a much taller felt on his knee, early 1900s.

right) was high style in the 1960s.

The advantage of the soft felt, besides its self-molding quality, was its ability to be worn with almost anything. Since men wore hats for all occasions—and all occupations—the soft felt was often chosen; it could be worn for informal occasions, for sport, for business, and for work. The derby symbolized the upwardly mobile middle-class, while the soft felt remained truer to its romantic origins—it is no accident that Indiana Jones wears a fedora (now displayed in the popular culture exhibit at the Smithsonian). The soft felt was worn by adventurers, gangsters, swingers, a more relaxed middle class, and—as a dress hat—by the working classes.

The soft felt continues to be worn for these same reasons; those who wear them are hip, carrying the combined connotations of all previous wearers. In an era of eclectic dress, the fedora can symbolize a range of social and occupational levels. If the bowler has gone the

5. How the Fedora Got Its "Snap"

These salesmen are twentieth-century men. They tell their stories of working in the hatting business, when all men wore hats and production was in the millions of hats per day. With hundreds of styles, colors, and finishes from which to choose, it was the hat salesman who was the link between the factory and the retailer. His aids were catalogues and sample hats, but his most important tool was his personal visit to the stores in his territory. A map cabinet once used by the Langenberg Hat Company contained drawers of maps, each drawer a different section of the country, each section with pin holes indicating a salesman's route and where he was to stop throughout his territory.

The hat samples he carried were the newest styles. Just as important, he also carried news of the latest fashions. Along with the suit salesman, he was the arbiter of fashion for the well-dressed gentleman. Retailers listened to the hat salesman, for the hat set the tone of an overall look.

Salesmen could be trained in a number of ways: through the company they represented, by fathers who were also in the hat business, or by other salesmen. Some salesmen became legends and were known across the country. They were the key speakers and demonstrators at sales meetings, and they were the inspiration to the younger men they trained.

Conversations with Hat Salesmen

Jack Lambert, Richard Pischke, John Secrest, and about Ken Jewell (deceased)

way of the entertainer, the fedora has been grabbed up by the person in the know.

Here are a few stories told by salesmen about their heroes and how they, as salesmen, came to learn their trade.

Jack Lambert

March 4, 1999, New York City
Jack Lambert was a vice-president of the John B. Stetson Company, owner of J. & J. Hatters in New York City, and now is a sales representative for Dorfman Pacific. He was trained by his father. Here is his story.

JL: In the old days all the hats were shown this way. They would have various crowns and different tapers and then different brims and different flanges. The actual shape of the brim might be more cuppy or go out further, and then, of course, they could finish them any way. Like this has a binding on it, but some would be finished raw, some would be welted up or welted down. Some would have rows of stitching to give strength to the hat, but this hat you can set up with a center crease in it. You'll see sheriffs will wear the hat that way [*shows how to shape a hat*]. You go in from the top and down. Of course, you can do this a lot better with steam. That would be your three-finger crease or cattleman's crease.

But then you can take the same hat—if you do, lower the back, round it out, pinch the front—you have that old-fashioned, what they called stratoliner look, which came in that funny-shaped box [*points to a variety of old boxes he has collected*]. You can shape that any way. All hats basically started this way—porkpie, diamonds. It's a lot easier if you take your stretching block. You turn this upside down on the stretching block that way and then you flip it back over and close the sides down on the block, and put it back up again, and then it pushes your top up.

Of course, you do this whole thing with steam while the hat is a lot softer. And if you do it real tight, you can get that edge right up against there like that, then it's called a tight telescope. The industry would call that a tight telescope, but the public calls it a porkpie—it's just like a newsboy cap. It's a better-sounding name to the public than any newsboy cap. And, of course, when you get done, you steam the top and just lay it flat, and flatten that top out completely. You could do different heights—the zoot suit guys would wear it way down

"Hat stores and hat etiquette are . . . things that are almost lost."

low—but it's the same hat: it's a dress hat.

Lowell Thomas used to buy this from us—he always wore this hat. He used to buy it from J. & J. Hat Center. In fact, his wife bought the last one he ever wore. I remember working with her.

You can take this back to 1981, and now you get your Indiana Jones. He didn't have the binding on the edge and he had a little different flange. Actually, it was the look of the 30s, which was a popular look back in the 80s. Of course, you can do the Montana crease. That's how they wore it in the United States. And then they would put their badge right there, or their scout medal, or their Park Service. And of course, the Canadians (the Royal Canadian Mounted Police), to be contrary, would use the same exact crown, but they would put the dip in the front [*points to hat*]. That's a real RCM hat and that's a real RCM band. That was loaned to me, because they're never allowed to give up their band. When they retire, they keep the band as part of the ceremony. But one of my neighbors' father was an RCMP and he lent me the band, but I had to promise to never lend it to anybody.

I got a ton of hats at home in my closet. You might want to mention in one of your stories—take big nails, like 6-penny nails, and nail them in the top of your closet all the way around. Then, instead of having the hats on the shelf where people throw their gloves and scarves and all the junk, and the hats go all misshapen—instead, when you get home, you just reach up. You can reach pretty high with a hat because it gives you another ten inches in height. I've got hats in every closet in the house, all the way around the top, old hats and hats my wife keeps yelling at me to get rid of. It's a nice way to store.

It's like caps. You do it like this in a restaurant, so it slides right into your pocket without hurting the visor. And I've shown that to a hundred dealers and they go, "Why didn't I ever think of that?" Hat stores and hat etiquette are all things that are almost lost.

DH: Tell me about your father.

JL: My dad was born in 1914. He had several different jobs, but when he retired from Stetson in about 1985 or

> "*A lot of very famous people [wore Stetsons]. If you could become a Stetson rep, that was really considered to be the best job you could have in the headwear business.*"

'86, he had been with Stetson for forty-one years. He was a senior sales representative. He was a typical traveling salesman. He was president of the Salesmen's Association in 1967. It was the largest attended dinner ever in the history of the Traveling Hat Salesmen's Association. As you probably know, the Traveling Hat Salesmen's Association is the oldest fraternal association in the world of its type. It's continuously had meetings for over one hundred years. My dad happened to be president that year. That was back in the days when it was held at the Waldorf Astoria, and everybody wore tuxedos. We have all these pictures of all these tuxedo-clad gentlemen. Each of the big companies would get a suite, all on the same floor (a floor that had just suites). And Stetson would have its own suite. My dad, because he was the New York guy, would be there.

There were a lot of very famous people associated with Stetson at that time. One of my dad's friends was Joe Gilidoe. He was one of the owners of the Brooklyn Dodgers. Stetson hat people, back in the days when Stetson was in its glory, were notorious people. They were involved in many, many famous things and ownership of other things. They were considered to be wealthy people, considered to be top of their career. If you could become a Stetson rep, that was really considered to be the best job you could have in the headwear business.

That was in the days when I'd go out with my dad when I was a kid. Literally, he would "make" New York. That's the expression—"make a state." I'd go up with him for the month of August and we'd make New York. That was back before there was a thruway. We'd get out in the car, and we'd load it up with hat tubes, and racks, and everything else. We would drive up north from New York. And you'd go to Poughkeepsie, then you'd go up to Albany, and then you'd work across to Utica and Binghamton, and all these towns. You'd do the upper tier and the lower tier.

We would set up every day or every two days in a hotel, depending on how many accounts were in the area.

All the variations of the snap-brim fedora style seen from the 1920s to the mid-1960s. "What was once the most casual of hats is now the most dressy style you can expect to see today. Variations in crown shape and height and brim width and hat-band width were repeated throughout the period during which such hats were worn, so that it is difficult to determine the dates for each hat."—John McMicking, hat maker

And the customers would come to us. We would set all the hats up just like a showroom, and then we'd sleep in the same room. So we'd have to take them all down at night and move them out of the way so we could fit on the beds.

Then my dad would have appointments set up. Kleinhans was in Buffalo, which was the biggest hat account in the northeast part of the country (they peaked out buying three million dollars worth of hats a year).

By virtue of osmosis I learned a lot about hats when I was a little kid.

Then at night we would go and watch the International League baseball games because all of those cities had minor-league teams. My dad was a Brooklyn Dodgers fan. He was born in Brooklyn. He came from the old school—an old Irishman. He wore a hat all his life, and he's the one that told me most of the hat stories, because most of the good parts of his life were in the hat trade.

I was very fortunate because he brought me to Philadelphia when Philadelphia was a working factory. There are not a lot of people who got to do things like that. I did not get to California, but he did, and he brought back pictures of Henry Stetson's ranch and the world's largest outdoor pool. He also has pictures where the John B. Stetson ship sank off the coast of California.

Also, his contacts—he knew all the best hat people all over the country. As I grew up and I'd go on a trip myself, he'd say, "When you're out in California, you've got to see Bill Mitre." And I'd go visit Bill Mitre, and Bill would have ten hat stories or twenty hat stories. They'd regale you all night or as long as you'd listen, because there weren't a lot of young people that were curious about the hat business. It was at a time when hats were waning in popularity. We've always had a niche trade, a niche business that a lot of people didn't get involved in. I wound up being very fortunate.

When we were kids we'd go to Candlewood Lake for the summer. We'd go up there for a month. Why did we go to Candlewood Lake? Because it's right near Danbury. My dad could work out of Danbury, use the phones over there and make his calls and do whatever he had to do. He'd rent a little cabin that I thought was the Taj Mahal, but when I went back and looked at it later in life it was just this little shack. For my dad it was just working for the company, just out of a different location. In August we'd go and sell hats. Those were my summers growing up.

DH: What was his name?

JL: Jack—John J. Lambert. Those were all good years and we were very fortunate to get around and see a lot of the hat business.

Richard Pischke

March 10, 1999, Philadelphia
Richard Pischke retired in 1998 after serving as sales representative for the John B. Stetson Company in New York City and Philadelphia. Richard was trained by the company and their senior salesmen.

DH: How did you get started?

RP: There were four good salesmen in the office who were responsible for New England out-of-town accounts. I was responsible for working with the out-of-town buyers who were unannounced. They came in from all over. It gave me an excellent opportunity to learn what was selling in Dallas, in California, in Alabama, and so forth. We'd get them from all over, international as well, overseas.

I had to maintain the office. I don't mean run it, I mean house clean, make sure things were in order. I worked for a vice-president, Earl Stevenson, who was the New York sales manager, and a very, very meticulous man, and a great guy to train with. He was a tremendous teacher.

After I got to learn and know the product in the training office, I'd go out with another salesman like Ray Curley, who was another great hat man, a

> "When I said Dick Pischke from Stetson Hat—every time the door opened. Stetson Hat was a magic name."

perfectionist. Ray taught me how to travel. We'd go to Albany today and Schenectady. He taught me the ins and outs of the road. He was great.

I guess it was 1954, after I had a year and a half in New York. There was a territory open in Philadelphia. A gentleman retired and they asked me if I would be interested. Of course, I knew the product. It was only a matter of moving home. It was the corporate office, Philadelphia, so I was right there.

DH: It's mostly gone.

RP: It wasn't much better then. It was pretty rough. You didn't see the factory, but you've seen pictures of the factory.

They had a beautiful sales office there, executive dining room, the hospital, and the building and loan with all those other benevolent things that John B. did for the people.

So I guess I started there in '54 with my own territory. It was a great experience because I saw the hat from the back shop to the packing—the whole nine yards—the making of the hat, the credit department, the customer service. I was really grounded well. They taught me well all the phases of the business.

It was a great experience, those years at the factory. There were just two of us; Bill Davies and myself split the accounts in this area. I think we did about a hundred miles around Philadelphia. Today in the hat business you have to do China and Russia to make a living. Philadelphia had the largest retail corner in the world at that time, even bigger than New York. It was on 8th and Market. On one corner there was Lit Brothers, an old department store we sold. Another corner was Gimbel's, a department store we sold. You've heard of them. And the third corner was Strawbridge and Clothier, which we sold. So this was the largest retail corner—not just hats, but retail.

When the temperature in the summer got to ninety degrees, whether it was July or August, the union shut down the back shop [the first stage of the hat manufacturing process where the raw fur is formed into cones and then steamed into the rough hat shape]. All those guys in the back—even at nine o'clock in the morning, they just couldn't handle it, no air conditioning.

I worked with Jack's [Lambert] dad, John. John was one of the salesmen in the New York office as a trainee. Bob Blanke was another. Bob was from Connecticut. He was well grounded. His father started in South Norwalk. He was a hatter, a union guy from South Norwalk. Bob was a salesman with us. John Lambert was a great salesman. He had it together, always thinking—send out a brochure here, a brochure there. He was ahead of his time. He was great.

These salesmen were the legends. Earl Stevenson, who was the vice-president of the sales office, came from San Francisco, a Philadelphia man. He took over for another legend, Joe Gilidoe. That goes back. Joe Gilidoe—I knew Joe—I met him a couple of times. They were the old legends; I was twenty-two years old. Those guys were sixty at that time.

DH: I have been told that the hat sets the tone in a men's department. When you were selling these stores, was this the case?

RP: That's 100 percent correct. The hat department was right up there with the clothing department. It wasn't perfume or shirts or ties. It was well thought of then.

The advantage with a hat was when you sold it, for whatever price, you didn't have to shorten it; you didn't have to lengthen the sleeve. You rarely saw it back.

In all the years, I don't think I've been in ten stores or made ten calls to a prospect, cold calls, or even to an established account, that when I said Dick Pischke from Stetson Hat —every time the door opened. Stetson Hat was a magic name. It's an unbelievable name.

The other funny story that goes back is when I was on the Eastern Shore, which is about 150 miles below here, a little town called Pokomo City. I was very new, a rookie, so to speak. I had a date with this man. Another salesman who was there was introduced as so-and-so of Chesterfield Hats. This was an older man, well dressed. I said, "Chesterfield Hats? I don't think I know Chesterfield Hats." He looked me right in the eye and said, "Brother, I can't be responsible for your ignorance." I learned where Chesterfield Hats were from; they were made over in Richmond at the time. I knew Chesterfield Hats after that!

DH: Did you get any of the account?

RP: As it turned out, he had to buy Chesterfield Hats because it was a less expensive hat, a lower end hat. Mine was a better hat. At that time, they ran Champ or Chesterfield or Baltimore (there was one out of Baltimore), because they had to have two lines—a less expensive line and a better line. Normally, we were the better line, or Knox was a better line or Dobbs was a better line, or Cavanaugh. The less expensive line was Chesterfield (Chesterfield was local, in that area) and Champ. Champ, made here in Philadelphia, was a very powerful competition.

Adams was on the downhill side of the mountain at that time, but Champ put out a hat for $7.50 in a single box. They were powerful at that time. George Goldberg sold Champ hats against me, but at the end he was vice-president for Stetson. He retired ten years ago. He ran the New York office at the end. Jack Lambert knew him well. Champ was out of Philadelphia. They were the Seleske Brothers.

Traveling got so expensive. Now we also do trade shows. Vegas is for dress hats; Denver is more western. That's a biggie. They get them from all over the country. We run one show twice a year in this area. It's called the King of Prussia Show outside Philadelphia. It ranks up in the top five or six shows in the country. We run it in August for next year's straws and in January for felts. It's organized by Stanley Expo Exhibits out of El Paso, Texas. It's got to be about forty years old. We started in a motel and people would go from room to room. It's grown to a big thing in the Sheraton Center. They do major volume. Everybody's there in the western business, plus horse equipment.

The way business is today, with the prices of traveling, shows are an integral part. You can write $100,000 or $50,000 at a show in three days. It may only be three dozen or two dozen accounts, but it means you don't have to travel thirty miles up in New York State. It's an integral part of doing business today. Of course, your management doesn't like it—they want you in the stores.

John Secrest

March 21, 1994, Tuscon, Arizona
John Secrest, another legend, had a brother, Ozzie, who was also in the hat business. Ozzie Secrest worked out of San Francisco and John was in Denver at that time. Earl Stevenson of the New York office hired Ozzie. John Secrest worked for the John B. Stetson Company.

DH: How long were you with the Stetson Company?

JS: I've been with them since 1939, and I've been retired eleven years.

DH: How did you get involved with the Stetson Company?

JS: Well, when I was growing up, I was a musician, and going to school and playing dance jobs at

John Secrest

odd times. We had our own band. Eventually I ended up with a band called Ted Weems. I don't know if you've heard of him; Perry Como would sing and I did that to work my way through college. And a very dear friend of mine was the vice-president of the Stetson Company. I got talking to him one day and said I was tired of traveling and one-night stands. He said, why don't you come around with me and let's go over to that Stetson place. I was with them for about a year and a half as a trainee. Then I started with the regular company and I've been with them ever since.

I started out as a salesman on the road—the San Francisco area, and then I went and worked the Denver territory. [I was] very conscious of the cowboys and how they raised themselves: the cattle, the hats. After about ten or twelve years I got into the designing of hats: western mostly; I also do dress. I did that on the side for a while and then did that with the company. The company at that time was in Philadelphia. I was a Denver boy by then, so I was quite a commuter. I would commute to Philadelphia as a designer. [I] did that for several years and then got into the national sales company; then for the last fifteen years I was with Stetson as head of design and sales.

DH: How did you get into the Hollywood end of it?
JS: The Hollywood end of it was strictly with the western. I didn't do too much with the dress hats. We started getting calls from them about the different type of hats they needed for pictures. Whatever was coming up, whether it was a Wayne picture or not—there are so many of them. I could hardly name all the stars. Practically all of them wore Stetsons. So I got into it with that. They'd give me an idea of what the story line was and what era it was. Some of the pictures they had! They didn't realize that for Indian fights and stuff before 1865, Stetson wasn't even in business then. Nor was there a "Stetson hat," because Stetson was actually the one that built the hat. I got commutin' out there quite a bit, with a few western cowboys and a few cowgirls. So that's the story of how I really got started. There were so many different types of hats that they wanted and you really had to go out there most of the time to see just what they were planning on doing.

DH: Did you go on the set and talk to the director?
JS: Actually it was more before the set, talking with the director before the set ever got up. He'd tell me the shoot was over in Utah or Colorado, when they were shooting the picture. Anyway he'd give me a year or so: "1890, 1895."

DH: What hats did cowboys wear before Stetson—if they were shooting a picture, say, before 1860?
JS: Before that there was really more or less dress hats or Derbies, crazy-looking things. There was mostly city people coming out in those days and they weren't real cute cowboys. A lot of them wore coonskin caps like Daniel Boone. They wore those quite a bit—anything to cover the head. Some of them just wore bandannas

around their head. Some of them went bare-headed; rain and sun would hit them. They had to have some kind of covering. Pretty miserable.

DH: Because the weather was so bad.

JS: Yes.

DH: They wore mostly European hats. The immigrants were wearing hats they wore in Europe.

JS: That's right.

DH: As a costume maker, I'm interested in what the directors told you.

JS: Right.

DH: Gary Cooper?

JS: William Holden or whatever.

DH: You go back to your office. How do you make that hat?

JS: Sometimes I'd do it just over the phone and they describe it to me and I'd send maybe a couple of models out to them. And you start out right from the very beginning. I only got the hat as it was finished off from the back shop, which is where they actually make the hat. It takes forty-four steps to make a single hat.

DH: Was it fun to work with Hollywood productions?

JS: Oh yes, yes. You get to know them pretty well and you're doing something for them which they appreciate. Trying to make something especially for them. I really never had a problem with any of them, even to a man.

DH: Were there any directors you worked with?

JS: I met [John] Ford several times. I really didn't meet them too much unless a new star was coming in and he didn't really have any idea of what kind of hat. Then you meet the director and he gives you the idea of what was wanted. But a regular cowboy comes in the pictures all the time. They'll tell you what they want for this type of picture, and what color hat they wanted—if they wanted to be a bad man with a black hat or a white hat.

DH: It was more the actor and not a costume designer that talked to you?

JS: Right. With these new actors, a lot of the time, the director or costume designer would say, "This is the look

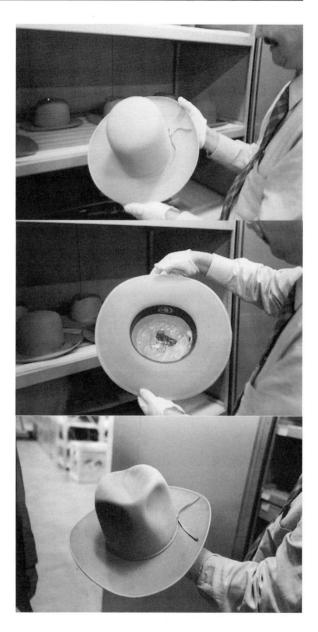

Hats from the collection of George Stetson donated to the Gene Autry Western Heritage Museum and displayed by curator James Notage.

we want—dirty, filthy clothes. We want a hat to look like he's worn it for thirty years"—that type of thing—and you'd beat it up and show it to them and they'd say, "Put some more dirt on it."

Before I left the company I had Don Williams, the country singer. He came to see me. He's been wearing this old Stetson hat for ten or fifteen years and it was beat up and he's known by it. [It] has this band on it with two buttons and turned up in the back. He went out in the factory with me. He didn't want the new hat, he wanted the new hat to be just like his old one. So we take a nice hat and just start beatin' and stompin' it on the floor, getting it dirty. But it ended up looking almost identical to his old hat he's been wearing. He's known by that hat—a character hat—and that's the way it is.

DH: Who supervised the rest of the costume?

JS: Most [of it was] by the costume department. They'd have some things in there, not guns, just clothing. They'd rearrange and put fuzz coming off the elbows to give them the hue that they wanted. I didn't meet too many—I used to meet a few boot people out there, like John Justin. He'd come out to make a few boots, and Luchaise, not a well-known name, a quiet name, the most expensive boot made. Custom boots for the different stars. I'd talk to them.

DH: Your hats were for the stars. The run-of-the-mill cowboys, where did they get their hats?

JS: They just got regular hats.

DH: They were probably in stock.

JS: That's right.

DH: At the studio.

JS: Right. There were a lot of western hats sold out there by specialty stores. Strictly cowboys who were movie stars. And you could go out there for half an hour and stand in our stores and see half the town.

DH: There's a store locally that shapes hats for their customers with a steamer.

JS: Most hats in good cowboy stores will not have even a crease in them; they'll just be round, and they shape it for the individual guy the way he wants it.

DH: Did William S. Hart shape his own hats?

JS: Yes. They'd shape their own [from] a regular open crown. Here's William S. Hart [showing pictures]. We would send it to him with the curl on the very end; that's terribly hard to do without a machine, so we'd send them to him that way. And Tom Mix's—we sent all his hats with an open crown, all of them. He used to travel to Europe quite often and he had thirty, forty hats he'd take with him to give away to people. He'd give a Stetson to the King of Siam or all his hosts.

DH: Here's a picture of John Wayne in *Stagecoach*.

JS: Here's one where he's wearing a flat crown. They're simple to put in. They're what's called a telescope crown.

DH: Earlier western hats had wider, floppier brims.

JS: Yes, they were using them for the elements in those days, trying to keep cool. They were much bigger hats in those days. As the general public got into Jeeps, [those] controlling cattle got smaller hats. In those days there were a lot more seven-inch crowns and four-inch brims. I've got a little book that shows that. This is a little Stetson catalogue. All the stores used them in the old days—you see the bigger brim and all open crown.

Ken Jewell

Ken Jewell was one of the legends. He ran the Cavanaugh store in New York City and was sales representative for the Resistol Hat Company. Here are a few stories told by a man trained by Ken, Bob Posey. Bob Posey was with the Resistol Hat Company for over thirty years and is currently with Hatco, manufacturer of Resistol and Stetson hats.

DH: Tell me about Ken Jewell.

BP: I have a special fondness for him. I'm just going to touch on something. In modern days, he probably knew the carriage trade better than anybody. I was lucky enough, and I say lucky, that John Milano was my men-

Ken Jewell

"*It was phenomenal the way he held and caressed the hats. He treated them like jewels, no pun intended.*"

tor for twenty-some years. And I worked with three guys mainly—Ken Jewell, John Milano, and another guy named Bernie Venner.

Bernie pioneered the West for Harry Rolnick. Harry Rolnick founded this company [Resistol]. He was a real character. There are so many funny stories about him, but he wasn't just a character. He was impressive.

DH: What hat stories would you like to be saved?

BP: Ken Jewell was an incredible man and the ultimate gentleman. He was also a phenomenal joke teller, who could do all the dialects. He had timing. You'd really see him. He would be acting them out and all this stuff. In fact, he was so good at his presentation when he would present a hat. It was phenomenal the way he held and caressed the hats. He treated them like jewels, no pun intended. The western salesmen, who really are a different breed, liked his presentations. They would marvel—what a guy, what a presenter, and what a man of integrity, and what a sense of humor. And it's all true.

I was lucky to have known him.

When he ran the Cavanaugh store in New York, it was the most prestigious store in the world, probably. And his customers were Crosby, Sinatra, Dutch Schultz the gangster, the Prince of Wales. Cardinals were his customers.

There was a theatricality about him. It's almost like when I was a kid and seeing a magic show, you were thrilled at witnessing this because it was special.

DH: That is what we hear from everyone. Historically, gentlemen hat makers were always in a class by themselves, starting with the felt hat makers' guild in the sixteenth century.

BP: Quality was always important. Here are some ads for Churchill hats. Ken Jewell and Churchill. The carriage tade acrried Oxford suits. A sport jacket today runs about $1,700. One of the criteria for a store carrying Churchill hats was that it has to carry Oxford suits. Ken had the humor, education, and knowledge to carry this all off. Even today when you go to dinner and mention his name, people beam.

6

The Disposable Straw

> "Miss Betsy Metcalf, at the age of twelve, without previous instruction, succeeded in making from oat straw, smoothed with her scissors and split with her thumb-nail, a bonnet of seven braids with bobbin inserted like open work, and lined with pink, in imitation of the English straw bonnets, then fashionable, and of high price. It was bleached by holding it in the vapor of burning sulphur. The article was much admired, and many came from neighboring towns to see it, and to order bonnets for themselves, at half the price of the imported."[1]—J. Leander Bishop, *A History of American Manufacturers*

Straw hats were the most versatile hats made. Woven in every style in which a felt hat was blocked, they were the corresponding summer head covering for males. If a man wore a felt bowler in winter, he wore a straw one in summer. He could wear a straw top hat if he liked, and wear it with his riding breeches.[2] As can be seen in the Taylor Brothers catalogue for 1889 (reproduced on the next two pages), hats made of straw were produced in farmer, boater, western, Homburg, wide-brimmed Cambridge, Shaker, and children's sailor or bonnet styles.[3] Straw hats were worn by everyone—young and old, male and female, rich and poor—because they were inexpensive and serviceable.[4]

Production of straw plait (braid) first began in the United States in 1798 after a long history in Italy, where the finest Leghorn straw was grown. A well-documented incident indicates that Miss Betsy Metcalf started the production in the United States. Betsy Metcalf was interested in women's accessories, but the desire for head coverings affected both sexes.

The straw hat industry exploded in the nineteenth century when machinery was incorporated into the process. Miss Metcalf's straw-splitting fingernail was replaced with machines that wove the straw, sewed the strands together, bleached and blocked all manner and shapes of hats for both men and women.

There is no difference in either the basic production of male and female straw hats or the process that little Betsy Metcalf followed in 1798. Machines took the straw fiber, split it, and wove it into plaits. Many braid patterns are produced in many types and grades of straw, of which the choicest remains the Italian Leghorn.

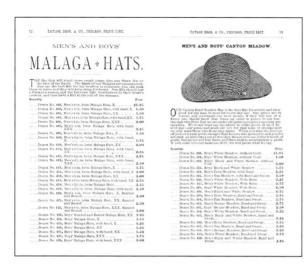
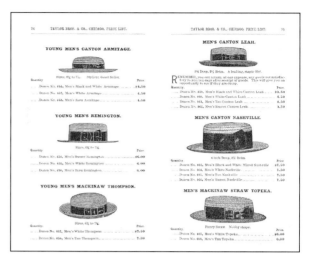
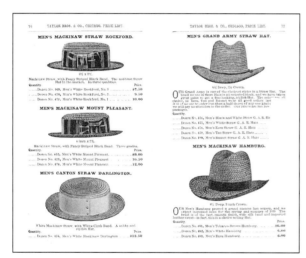

Pages 72–83 of the Taylor Bros. & Co. catalogue for Spring 1889. Page size is 4⅛ x 6⅝ inches.

6. The Disposable Straw

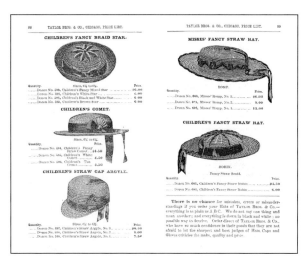
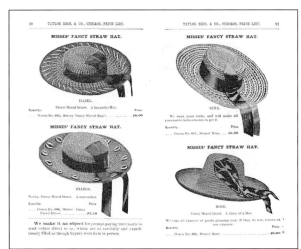
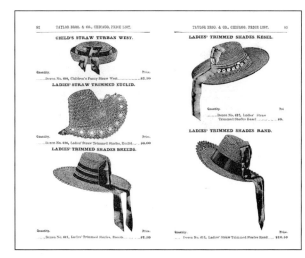
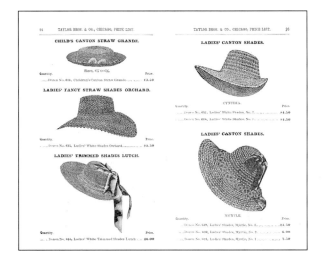
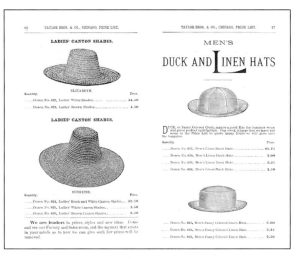

Pages 86–97 of Taylor Bros. & Co. catalogue for Spring 1889.

The shape in which the braids are ultimately sewn determines the style of the hat. Other popular straw hats came from China; they were made into what were called "White Canton Straw Hats." They were sold by the Sears, Roebuck Company and the Taylor Company in their nineteenth-century catalogues.[5] Panama "Harvest" hats are also mentioned.

The Panama straw hat has a long history in Latin America, dating back to the Valdivia culture in 4,000 B.C. A modern descendant is the popular summer Panama hat, now sold in select hat stores all over the world. Hat maker S. Grant Sergot explains that the Panama straws are "woven from finely selected 'Paja Toquilla,' a palmetto plant native to just Ecuador; they are supple and the most durable woven hat in the world. They are graded from one to twenty, in ascending order of quality and cost; the lower grades are *'selecto.' 'Fino'* begins at ten. Fourteen earns a *'finissamo,'* which is where the 'Montecristis' come in. Twenty qualifies as a *'fino fino.'*"[6] These differing grades are woven in Ecuador by craftspeople. Artisans can take up to six months to weave one Montecristi (the name of the town where the hat originated), while hats of average quality are woven by the hundreds of women who supply the bulk of the straw hat trade. Although the hats are made in Ecuador, the name "Panama" stuck because of their point of export, the docks of Panama.

The Montecristi has always been considered the prince of the woven straw hat. In a book dedicated to the complex story of the Panama hat, *Panama, a Legendary Hat*, Martine Buchet writes:

> The quality of a "fino" depends on the selection of the straw, the fineness of the weave and the regularity of the brim. It is judged by the quality of rows that make

up the crown of the hat, and finally, by the appearance of the finished product. The rows, which are arranged in concentric circles, starting from the center of the hat (called the "rosette"), can be made out when the hat is placed in front of a light. Their number, which is synonymous with a more or less serried weave, is an important indication of quality, when all other criteria have been satisfied.[7]

Throughout the twentieth century it was the Panama hat, purchased from elite men's stores and large retail outlets, that satisfied summer sartorial requirements. There were a number of distinct styles: "The best known was the 'Borsalino,' from the name of the celebrated Italian hat-maker who had invented its shape. Then there was the 'Stetson'. . . . But the 'planter' and 'colonial' styles were also popular. The most chic remained the so-called 'natural Panama,' which one shaped oneself, and whose form was never fixed once and for all. This required straw of high quality, which in general was only to be found with the 'Montecristis.'"[8] You can still find a J. C. Penny's brand Panama, mostly with the narrow brim of the 1950s, in flea markets and antique malls (sadly, the straw is often cracked), and sometimes, with luck, the still charismatic Montecristi. Men continue to wear Panama hats, as hat merchants will attest. Some merchants have become so intrigued with the hand-crafted Panama that they travel to Ecuador to purchase hats directly from their makers.[9]

The Panama had its rival—the straw boater. Originally it was a sailor's hat that was lacquered and modified by flattening the brim and crown.[10] Frank Whitbourn attributes the name of this hat to the painting *Three Men in a Boat*, by Jerome K. Jerome.[11] Another name for the flat straw was skimmer, a hat extremely popular with boys' and girls' schools (the Harrovians have their own distinctive wider brim). Photographs from the late 1800s through the mid-1900s show everyone wearing straw boaters while enjoying summer picnics and train rides or fashionably sauntering down city boulevards.

There were two types of summer boaters, recalls Helen Hollberg (who celebrated her ninety-fifth birthday in June 2001). She said that in the 1920s and 1930s you hardly ever saw a man without a hat:

> Most of my beaus wore straw hats. During this time there were two kinds of straw hats—the kind that were about three layers of straw thick and the ones that were a single layer. The single-layer type were known as "throw-aways," for the simple reason that men would buy them at the beginning of the summer season for, I think, around two dollars in the summer of 1920 and around $3.50 by the 1930s. Provided it did not look too shabby, they would wear it all summer. Perhaps they would buy two. But the fun thing was come Labor Day, no matter how new or how old, they would toss them

in the trash, to repeat the season's ritual again come June. Then hats seemed to disappear one day.[12]

The gentlemen shown in the illustrations above look ready to escort Helen anywhere.

Versatility was characteristic of the straw hat. The men in the photograph on the opposite page appear to feel properly and formally dressed for their photographs, even though they are not wearing suit coats. How a man wore his straw hat was as important as with any other hat. He could slant it or wear it sitting straight on his head. The wearer always had a choice, especially with the Panama's flexible shape. That was the convenience of the straw hat; it could be worn by children and adults, men and women, for relaxing or casual formality.

6. The Disposable Straw

6. The Disposable Straw

Conversation with John Milano

January 8, 1996, Garland, Texas

John Milano has been in the hat business all his life. He tells of his experiences with the companies for which he has worked, the products he has developed, and the people he has known. He now has his own company, Milano Hat Co., Inc., producing Justin brand, authentic western headwear.

DH: John, how did you start in business?

JM: In 1963 I moved to Texas from New York because Mr. Rolnick of Resistol decided to move the management of the retail division, which at that time did about two and one-half million worth. Texas was the headquarters of the company. So I was offered the opportunity to retain my job, which was director of the retail operation, or stay in New York and just handle those stores. I decided to move down here. Late in '63 I was made vice-president of the retail division. Then in 1967, December 27, Byer Rolnick was sold to Koret Corporation of California. In January of '68 I was asked to develop the merchandising department of Resistol, because of my experience in retail. I had the knowledge of what the consumer wanted, and they thought that I could help them in the merchandising. I held the dual capacity of supervising the retail division, concentrating on merchandising. In 1969 I found that doing both jobs was too much for me, and since retail was my first love, I decided to go back to retail full time. The young man I had taken with me out of retailing and into merchandising, Bob Posse, is the merchandiser of Resistol today. Then in 1973, following a couple of disastrous years for the company, I was offered the presidency of the company, which I took. In 1982 I took early retirement and started my own company.

DH: Did you start from scratch, or did you buy another company?

JM: No. No, I started from scratch. We started from scratch—the old building has 7,000 square feet of space. My desk, the secretary's desk (occupied by my wife), and an empty warehouse existed with plans for where the machinery would go. My obligation with Resistol ceased on April 1, and on April 3, I was in business.

DH: Were you set up to make straws or felt hats?

JM: Both, but primarily straws. The felt end, unless you have your own body plant, it is difficult to control your quality. I had the good fortune of being associated with a person, Harry Rolnick, who was, to me, the best hatter in the business; he was a totally quality-oriented individual. They made the finest hats in the world, and that was why they survived. I believe the John B. Stetson Company closed everything, and they licensed the Steven's Hat Company of St. Joe, Missouri, to use the Stetson name. Hat Corporation of America, which was a big company in 1972, was acquired by Resistol, which was a division of Kotacorp Industries. The only one of the old-timers left who were around with Resistol today is Langenberg, although under new management. That is the only company.

It also happens to be the oldest hat company in the United States—even older than Stetson. Now, the Langenberg Company today is somewhat different from what it was in the old days. In the old days, when Johnny Langenberg owned it, he made the best unbranded product. He was never interested in developing his retail trade with a brand and chose to do his business primarily through jobbers. That's one of the reasons, probably, that the company did not grow as fast as others. I remember when I was just starting in the business—I came to Texas one year—I went into Mr. Rolnick's office and I was introduced to Johnny Langenberg. It was about 1958, '59, late 50s, early 60s. Mr. Rolnick said, "You're meeting the only man that buys as much or more expensive Australian fur than I do." And in those days Resistol was a small company compared to Langenberg, but Mr. Langenberg and Mr. Rolnick were from the same school. They were hatters and were interested in quality, in developing a quality product. And I think it is one of the reasons the company, Resistol, survived. Langenberg is still Langenberg.

DH: Do you make your own hat bodies or do you get them from Resistol?

JM: No. The felt bodies—I import them from Portugal. Originally, when I first started the business, I got my bodies from South Africa. See, I had an advantage in starting my business—more than one. Number one, I was fortunate enough to have Mr. Rolnick as my mentor, who exposed me to the various facets in the hat business, because I ended up knowing how to sell hats—dress and cowboy hats. But then I ended up knowing what the component parts were, spending time in the factory. Then, as I became the merchandiser, I became the procurer of raw material. I was also involved in managing the overseas sales and licenses. So when I started my business, I went down to South Africa to visit my friends at Dorian hats with whom I had been working—as they were one of the Byer Rolnick licensees—and asked them if they would be interested in making some felt bodies for me to use in producing Milano Hats, which they did. Unfortunately, they went out of business in 1985. They sold most of the equipment to Stetson. Stetson brought it to their body shop in Norwalk, Connecticut. Then when Irving Joel was the owner of Hat Brands, he didn't buy Stetson, but the Stetson equipment and the license to use the Stetson name. He destroyed most of the machinery that he didn't need. Well, it was too expensive to ship it down to Texas.

It's unfortunate, but if you look at the history of the hat business, which I have learned in the last forty years, there has not been a piece of machinery made in the last one hundred years. When a small company went out of business, the manufacturers were going to buy the equipment and put it in the warehouse, and end up cannibalizing and using it for parts. Everyone had developed their own technology in machinery. I'll show you when we go back in the factory—for instance, a leather sewing machine that was made by Singer seventy-five years ago. I know when I was president of Resistol in 1980, I signed the biggest purchase order for parts on that machine, $250,000, to make us parts from Chicago so we could rebuild old skeletons that we had ended up with. Unfortunately, not only had he [Irving Joel] destroyed the equipment he didn't use, but he also bought the Doran Hat Company machinery, including all the blueprints to make machine parts.

We have today developed our own presses, which are completely different from what's in the industry. Fortunately for me, my son (who is not here today and is taking a well-deserved vacation) works with me. We were on a plane to Portugal and he said, "Dad, I've been

6. The Disposable Straw

John Milano holding one of his fur felt western hats.

> "*In straws . . . you're dealing with a product in which the finishing process allows you to obtain the level of quality that you want. It's controllable because of the raw material you start with.*"

working on a pressing machine." And he showed me a sketch he had made on the plane. I said, "OK, go ahead." Because he knows what he wants. When you're as small as we are, and you have to depend on other people to do work for you, you don't have the same flexibility. If I owned a full-fledged machine shop right here, then I could control my destiny. When you're dealing with other people, you're at the mercy of other people.

DH: He gave this sketch to a machine shop?

JM: Yes, and they made the component parts for us and then we assembled it.

DH: That gets tricky.

JM: Yes. We did the same thing when we started the company in 1983. My son, who was an electrician journeyman and made a lot of money, came to me and said that if he had to work for somebody, he might as well work for something that had his name on it. "That's OK with me," I said, "if you can afford to take a cut, because this company can't afford to pay you what you're making." He accepted. My oldest son gave me another pleasant surprise about three months ago. He's an attorney. He worked down in San Antonio. He decided he didn't want to live away from his family. He's going to move back to Dallas and join the company. He will prac-

tice some law to close his pending files. Richard is very well equipped in merchandising, designing, production, production control, and distribution. John, Jr. has more of the affinity of a salesman. And being a lawyer, he has enough BS in him to be a good salesman. That's what we're doing now.

DH: Are some of the better hat bodies coming out of eastern Europe?

JM: For dress hats.

DH: Not for western hats?

JM: No. No, you see, western hats—the process is the same, yet it isn't, because in making a dress hat you want a soft, luxurious feeling.

DH: Like Borsalino?

JM: No, no. Borsalino—even in Italy, Panizza and Barbisio made a much better hat. Today none of the three manufactures hats any more.

DH: Where were they located?

JM: Panizza was in Lago Maggiore. Barbisio was around the Lombardy area. I don't know if it was Milan or not. If you take an Italian dictionary and you look up hats, it will show Borsalino. And if you take the Webster dictionary, it will show Stetson—it's become synonymous with a western hat. It used to aggravate me when

From top: Straw hats prior to edge trimming; stacked straw hats prior to final blocking; finished straw hats.

I was at Resistol. Every time there was a dignitary coming to Dallas, the Chamber of Commerce asked us to donate a couple of hats, and they would present them as Stetsons. It used to aggravate the daylights out of me. Everybody refers to tissue as Kleenex—it's a generic term—you have to live with it.

DH: Did Stetson get popular by aggressive marketing?
JM: In late 1800, early 1900, Stetson was—John B. moved to the West for health reasons. He happened to discover the need for a wide-brim hat, which the pioneers began to wear because of the broader brim. If you look at movies, and look into Western heritage, you will find that Wyatt Earp didn't wear a big hat like was shown in the movies, because there were no big hats. Doc Holiday wore a Homburg. So most of your cowboy hats were these 2- and 2½-inch brim dress hats that were converted to cowboy hats by snapping the brim, which is today what we call the Australian outback look, and then that was the western look.

Stetson was the first company to make a western hat. I remember the eastern manufacturers—even during my tenure in the hat business, when I used to attend the hat conventions—the big shots from Hat Corporation of America, from Mallory, from Disney, and from Lee, all these companies, old companies, all looked down on the cowboy hats. Well, the cowboy hat is the only thing that sells today. You take the western business out of the hat business and you have no hat business. So for these reasons, Stetson was given more freedom, and the only competition they got with the western hats was from Miller Brothers Hat Company, Resistol, and Langenberg. They were making western hats. That was the only competition Stetson had.

In those days, the western hat business was not what it is today. I remember when I attended the first Resistol sales meeting in 1957, we had a sales meeting for three days. The last day, for two hours, only 25 percent of the salesmen held the western sales meeting. The western line consisted of what Resistol called the San Antonio, which was the Stetson "Open Road" or the

Borsalino "Allesandria"—lightweight, four line bands, open crown, silver body color. Then in the early sixties it became the LBJ because it was the hat that LBJ wore—except that he didn't wear it in a 3½-inch brim, he wore it in a 2⅞-inch brim. It was known in the industry by everybody as the southwest businessman's hat. Every banker, every doctor, every lawyer wore that hat. Johnson popularized it more. For instance, Resistol used to make the hats for President Johnson; they were so personalized that the lining in the hat, instead of having the brand, had the map of the State of Texas with a red star marking his ranch location and LBJ signed across it. Resistol made all the hats for him. Johnson had a small room that was like a hat store. Everyone who visited the ranch got a hat.

Stetson got out of the hat business in 1969 because the John B. Stetson factory was located smack in the middle of downtown Philadelphia. The land was worth a fortune, and the hat business by that time was already on the decline. They decided to shut down the factory, get out of the hat business, give somebody the name, license the name to somebody. The John B. Stetson Company remained, as a market entity, a licensor of its name throughout the world for headwear.

Then back in late 1970s, they ventured to license the name for other products—Cody perfume was one—cologne. Use it every morning and money bills come out of it. There was a change in the licensing management of Stetson and these young men came in. I believe one was out of CBS records and his reputation was in promoting the names. He was the one who put Stetson in with Cody Colognes. But then, during *Urban Cowboy*, he decided that the two to three million dollars he was getting from licensing the Steven's hat wasn't enough. He decided to buy the Steven's Hat Company and got back into manufacturing. That was the beginning of the end, because then they proceeded to file for bankruptcy sometime in the early 80s. That's when Irving Joel bought the Stetson Hat Company and combined it with Resistol.

DH: Now Hat Brands?

JM: The last public information was that they had a twenty-year licensing agreement to use the name and pay a royalty. After twenty years, they would own the trademark and stop paying royalties.

DH: What do you think of their quality now?

JM: The quality—any quality today is not as good as it used to be for many reasons. Chances are, if you had come here five years ago, instead of wearing a raincoat, you would probably have been wearing a fur coat.

DH: The problem is finding enough good fur?

JM: Well, see—fur for the hat business—nobody can afford to develop skins—rabbits, beaver, rabbits particularly, for the sole purpose of making hats. In the hat business, we used to buy the cheapest skins, the ones that the furriers didn't want. We bought the skins not by the piece, but by the weight. Because you take a skin, you clean it first, and take out all the long guard hairs, and then you shave the fur off the skin. You're only using somewhere between 12 percent and 13 percent of what you buy. In its first operation, when you shave the skin, when you clean the fur to form it into a hat body, you lose another 18 percent. You just can't afford to pay expensive prices. Resistol was one of the first companies to make high-priced beaver hats for the western industry. We used to buy pieces from the furriers. Then, the furriers bought prime skins. We took the scrap that was on the floor and we bought it for eight to nine dollars a pound. We took it, separated it by color and by size into strips, and made plates by gluing the pieces of scrap on a piece of brown paper. The plates then went through the process of shaving and cutting as if they were skins. You can't shave a small piece of skin. You need a piece big enough to do it. That's why the quality of the hat was what it was.

DH: Expensive labor?

JM: Very much so, very much so. Also because the furriers plucked the long hairs by hand, and did everything manually, you had a better product to work with. We had to bleach them to a more uniform color before cutting them. But every time that you bleached it, you took some strength out of the fiber by carroting the skins (a chemical we used to use in the hat business—used to be mercury—but then they stopped using it because of what it did to people). You put on this carroting chemical, then when it dries up, it sort of turns brownish. When you make a white hat using carroted fur only, unless you use a lot of powder in finishing it, you have a washed-out look because it's all the burned parts from the carroting.

A lot of things go into hat making. The best definition that I ever heard for the felt hat business is—it's a Black Magic business. There is never a time that you think you have conquered all the natural idiosyncrasies that can develop from a felt hat. Fur being a live fiber, it is affected by weather conditions even after it is made.

In straws it's entirely different, because you're dealing with either a natural fiber or a synthetic fiber. You're dealing with a product in which the finishing process allows you to obtain the level of quality that you want to get. It's controllable because of the raw material that you start with—I don't care what you do, this body doesn't change. It's a paper body; it doesn't change. Now what we make out of it when we finish it has a lot to do with what we do, the type of lacquer, if we dry it through an oven (you end up getting a yellowish cast on the hat; furthermore, you are destroying the fiber). If you dry them naturally, which is the way I like to do it, you have a better-quality product. You can control your destiny. The way you sew in the leathers, using leather instead of using plastic. There's a lot of things you can do in controlling the product you want to obtain. In felts, unless you start with a good body, forget it, it doesn't happen.

DH: Stetson uses synthetic paper. Do you manufacture it? Is it manufactured in Japan and hand-woven in China?
JM: It is—I know, I developed it. About in the mid-70s when western hats began to take off—in those days you used basically four different bodies. The Panama hats, which were woven in Ecuador, were made out of tequilla straw, which is a natural fiber. Then we had what we called "Formosans," made out of twisted coated-paper fiber, made in Japan and then woven in Taiwan. That is why we called it a Formosan. Then we had the "Philippine Bangkok," which is a natural rice fiber that's hand-woven in the Philippines. And then you had also what they called the "Devao Hemp" braid that made a uniquely strong woven hat. In the early 70s straw hats became cowboy hats and were getting popular. The available raw material became in short supply. Panama bodies, being a natural fiber, were limited as to the size body you could make; when 7-inch crowns, 4-inch brims became popular, you could not get a body big enough.

The tequilla straw that is used to weave Panama hats has only a small portion of long staple fiber, therefore limiting the production of large size bodies. The tequilla palm is like an artichoke; the finest fiber was in short supply, as you would find it near the bottom. When weaving fine-quality Montecristi Panama, a weaver would be compelled to make many splices in order to produce bodies large enough to make cowboy hats. To produce the less expensive hats, we used hat bodies woven in Taiwan using Marcus twisted coated paper in 8 to 10 and 12 Bu (the unit of measurement used by the Chinese to indicate fiber thickness). The yarn being continuous allowed the weaver to weave any size hat body.

During one of my annual trips to Hong Kong and Taiwan I asked one of our major suppliers, the Sunflower Mercantile Company, if the Marcus yarn could be made in 5 Bu (approximately 5mm) in an ivory color that would allow us to duplicate the weave and pattern of the Panama hats, which would give us unlimited supply at a lesser price. When Mr. Nixon opened the China market, we were able to weave some of these bodies in mainland China. At first we had some difficulties with the Chinese weavers because they were accustomed to weaving natural fibers and small bodies. Now we were asking them to weave hat bodies large enough to make cowboy hats and in synthetic (paper) yarn.

DH: How did they adapt?

Tex-Mex style straw with sombrero-sized brim

Mexican straw sombrero

JM: Very well, except they took three years, because they were not accustomed to making cowboy hats. They were accustomed to making dress hats. They made small capalinas (small caps), which was easy, but when we asked them to make a 6-inch crown or 6½-inch crown, they ended up making stove pipes. They didn't make it wide enough. Take a body like this, because this is hand woven, the tip of the crown measures 6 inches in diameter, then from here to the bend-line measures 5½ inches. From the bend line to the edge of the brim is 5 inches. You can make any hat, any size, any count, except up to 7¾. If you go to 7⅞, you need a larger body. But because the body is woven by hand, you can stretch it this way, you can stretch it that way, you can do anything you want with it. And being a man-made fiber, it doesn't break. This allows you the flexibility of anything you want.

DH: So it took three years to get them to do it right?

JM: Yes, the first one that really took off is the first one I showed you. The first hat bodies were 2 x 2 and 1 x 1 weave—1 x 1 means that the fiber is woven one strand on one strand; 2 x 2 is woven two strands on two strands.

DH: Like a twill weave pattern?

JM: Now that hat [*holds up hat*] is still our number-one seller in the industry.

DH: This is made from your basic body?

JM: Yes, but when we introduced that hat, we were selling it for fifteen dollars. Today we're selling it for thirty-two dollars.

DH: Not bad?

JM: No, it isn't, but the problem we are having is the shrinking of the Chinese weaving industry.

DH: And the price will go up?

JM: It is extremely difficult today to get them to make a 5 Bu. To translate, to understand, the fiber is 5mm. They made 7 and 8mm, but originally we started with the 5mm. Then there became a need for finer hats. First we made a 3 Bu, which is our Imperial Shantung. This is a 2 Bu in a 1 x 1—very fine.

DH: It's almost on a level with Montecristi.

JM: Yes, but better, because that hat will never break. This is a Montecristi that I decided to wear on the golf course. I banged my head on the cart, and it cracked. It is an 18-grade Montecristi. This hat, when I was running the retail division, we were retailing it for $120.

DH: That is a lot to lose. This is more flexible.

JM: It won't break. Literally, you can sit on it. And if you have wrinkles in it, you can reblock it, and it will be one piece again. That business is impossible to maintain. We developed that grade of hat; as small as we are, we probably do a disproportionate amount of business in that hat.

DH: Is it too exacting a type of work?

JM: It's very bad on your eyes because of the very strict quality control that we have. I have these samples because every time I give them an order, I have them make samples before they ship the order. We don't make anything to stock. Everything we make is made against a customer order.

DH: How does Christy in England operate?

JM: Christy, the whole English hat business, went to hell in a basket long before it went in this country. The English gave up on it and started to make cloth hats—the Rex Harrison hats. The English are buying from Portugal, Czech Republic, or Hungary, and other Eastern countries.

DH: Do you use hare fur from the meat industry?

JM: I don't know what they're doing with Belgian hare, because they're not making felt bodies.

DH: Very few.

JM: Failsworth was the only one. Christy is part of HBHM. I've been through HBHM. If you've been through these factories, you saw how antiquated they are. I'll never forget, Failsworth was our licensee for the Dobbs division. I went to the factories. Here in the United States we're accustomed to the back shop that makes the bodies, starting with the fur, ending up with the rough body. And the bodies go to the front shop. The bodies come out of the body room and come out finished hats in boxes. I went to these factories, and they started up here, and went down there, and then over here.

DH: They're using 1880s factories. How about in Italy?

JM: In Italy they were doing it; but, again, Italy was a small market. Again, you have 250 million people here. You watch movies that were made in the 30s and 40s, and you never see anyone without a hat, male or female, which is the exact opposite of what you see today. Being a native Italian, from day one, I was fortunate to have a lot of exposure with Americans, starting with the GIs. I had the distinction of starting the first shoeshine parlor in my town, and proudly stated that I shined the shoes of the Fifth Army.

DH: What town?

JM: Sorrento. I watched American movies, read American magazines. That's how I learned to speak English. I always found the American market and business methods unique. I remember sitting at the top licensee in Italy, Panizza, and a gentleman by the name of Antonio Gamba, probably the most educated hatter in the world—everywhere in the world, if you mentioned Tony Gamba, everyone knew who you were talking about—he was the president of Panizza, and had a doctorate in the felting process. OK. There is a logic to the felting process of a dress hat. I remember during *Urban Cowboy*, business was so good in cowboy hats, I didn't want to waste time in dress hats, so I went to Europe and I had dress bodies made for me in Europe. We also found in those days, because of the strong influence of *Urban Cowboy*, a new market had opened which we chose to call at the time, transition market. The hippies in New York and the eastern cities wore funny cowboy hats. They wore the same hat, except it was not the 4-inch brim; the 3½-inch crown was shifted frontally, and most of the time it had big feathers all over it. Those bodies didn't have to be as good, so we had them made overseas. But because you were dealing with a cowboy hat, you needed more stiffening in the brim.

When I told Tony Gamba the amount of stiffening to put in the brim—I made the sin, the ultimate sin, of telling him to put stiffening in the crown—we had the biggest argument. And Tony could be quite a dictator. I had been brought up to respect my elders, until he insulted my intelligence. Then I said, "Tony, let me tell you something. I give you credit for what you know in the felting process and your tremendous expertise in hat making." I said, "The reputation you have is well founded, no one is second to you. But, Tony, when it comes to making cowboy hats, you don't know from Shinola—OK?—so don't tell me. Tony, Penizza is dying. You're making 300 hats a day. I make 600 hats an hour. You're going bankrupt; I'm running 16 percent overrun. We're growing, you're dying. Put your pride aside. You need production in the body shop. Can you make me 100 dozen a day? 1,200 pieces a day? Yes, that's what I mean, 1,200 pieces a day. You can have all or part of it. Tell me what you want, and I'll make it very easy for you. You're going to make a black and a brown." He couldn't believe it. And then when he came over and I took him through our factory, and I showed him the finished product, all of a sudden he understood where we were coming from. That was the problem.

DH: To stay in business, then, you need to change and keep developing.

JM: If you want to stay ahead, otherwise you stay in the status quo. We developed the Shantung; all of a sudden, without the Shantung you'd have no straw hat business.

DH: Right, because you just can't hand-weave straw bodies or they cost $4000 like the Montecristis Milton Johnson sells in Santa Fe.

JM: I know Milton is a hell of a promoter. The hats in his shop, the non-Montecristis, I make most of them. The finest Montecristi you can buy today is a 20 count, a 20/21 body. In a western hat you can get up to a 30. I don't know what you would put in a hat to make it worth $4000. I'll show you an example. During the *Urban Cowboy*, the Xs marked quality. 10X was a fifty-dollar hat. Then the same body, packaged and trimmed differently, became a beaver 100 and that was the top of the line. I'm talking about Resistol in those days. The 7X, the 10X, the beaver 100 were all exactly the same hat, they're all 100 percent beaver. The only difference was in the leathers used and the trim used and the packaging. Beaver 100 came in a suitcase [points] right here; when *Urban Cowboy* took over, we went from a smooth leather to a nylon calf leather substitute. But this was the only difference, and the leather was the only difference.

In those days, the *Urban Cowboy* was such a fad that the sky's the limit, and every year we were called upon to do something different. The first thing we did, we developed a Black Gold. There was a lot of expensive dark colored fur that we couldn't use for anything. We made the Black Gold [holds up hat]. This is the prototype for the Black Gold—best one that was ever made. The difference in these hats, besides the color, is the suede finish on it. There's a store in Dallas called Cutter Bill's. Cutter Bill's was really the front runner of developing the "Urban Cowboy" concept, even before the *Urban Cowboy* movie. The merchandiser and buyer was a young man by the name of John Pierce, who is now the merchandising director of the Justin Boot Company. John was a young man who came up with the concept, because the western industry was not developing anything but shirts with fringes and yokes. He would bring in something different. He came to me every year and said, "John, we have to do something different." This was the white ermine, ermine fur [*holds up white hat*]. This hat was delivered to Cutter Bill's in a Brinks truck. This hat retails for $2000. This is a vicuna hat [*holds up hat*]. There's less than 3 percent vicuna in that; most of it is beaver. Here's a "Touch of Mink," literally a touch. And this was a natural beaver hat.

DH: When you say natural, is that the natural color?

JM: Yes, no dyeing, natural brown.

DH: Where do the beavers come from?

JM: In the United States.

DH: Do they still trap beaver?

JM: Yes, not now as much as they used to, but that was a big business. This was a "second" [*holds up hat*]. These hats would not be shipped to a customer. This was a beaver 100. Most customers today would give their eyetooth to get these hats—that's first quality.

DH: Are these all your hats?

JM: Yes.

DH: Did you know Ken Jewell?

JM: Ken Jewell was the president of the Churchill division of Byer-Rolnick. Ken was in the business about sixty years. Ken was born February 15, 1909. He was a fantastic person, and had tremendous stories about the hat industry.

[*Ken Jewell is discussed in more detail in Chapter 5.*]

7

A Chap and His Cap

"Caps, Caps, Read All About 'Em!
Those jaunty visored newsboy hats, popularized by such dubious style makers as Valerie Bertinelli on
"One Day at a Time," Paul Simon in his "Say, Say, Say" video, the boxer Jerry Cooney and,
oh, newsboys, are back. This season, the chipper chapeaus have found new fashion status on the
glamorous heads of Jennifer Lopez and Chloe Sevigny, in the advertisements for Louis Vuitton and
Bottega Veneta, and on runways in shows like Emanuel Ungaro's this month in Paris.
Thus the newsboy hat joins the peasant blouse and the messenger bag as fashion items that exceed the
incomes of their namesakes."—*New York Times,* Sunday, March 25, 2001

Whether plaid fabric, wool tweed, linen, corduroy, or cotton, the cap has a myriad of uses. In 1924 the Davis & White Spring/Summer Catalogue described the model called the "Limited" as "a cap designed especially for the tourist or any outside use. Made of khaki cloth in drab color. Extremely serviceable. Delivered to You for ......$1.00." For winter, Davis & White added flaps to the cap, called it the "Rite Style," and described it as "a classy dress cap that is both warm and stylish. All wool, neat patterns, made in one piece top, good weight, fur inbands. You will like it. Delivered to You for .... $1.00."[1] The cap was an all-weather accessory, lasting throughout the twentieth century.

Golfers still wear caps on the fairways. My university department chairman dons his every winter. One could link the cap to the baseball cap, jockey cap, cricketer's cap, for they all have sewn fabric, round crowns, and a partial front brim. The shape of the knit tam o'shanter resembles the puffy round crown, yet has no brim, like sailor hats and berets. The cap has both crown and partial front brim, which change according to fashion and purpose.

Hatters said the cap spread as democratically as the bowler.[2] Fashion plates show men wearing caps for motoring and traveling. Often the cap was made of linen to match the linen duster. The cap was a head covering that could be worn anywhere men gathered informally.

A series of smaller sized caps are illustrated in the 1887 Sears, Roebuck & Co. catalogue. They were sold in a "fancy mixed cassimere" which was "extra well

A generic cloth cap worn by a young gentleman. He wears a patterned wool cap, wool tweed jacket, and print tie. The cap is slightly tilted, worn above his forehead.

Fashion plate showing men dressed for travel.

This cap's broader crown suggests that it dates from the 1920s, when crowns were at their fullest. Actually this cap was made in the 1950s and proportioned to earlier dimensions.

made and nicely lined" and came in "assorted dark and medium colors." They called this particular style a golf cap. They also sold "navy blue broadcloth golf caps, navy blue fine ribbed corduroy and a beautifully drab shade"of cap. For the more style conscious, Sears carried "fancy corduroy golf caps of extra fine quality with leather sweat bands and beautiful silk lining. Dark blue with an artistic silver fawn mixture of small specks, forming a truly beautiful combination."[3] These extra quality caps also came with a satin lining for the same price.

Boys could choose from "Boy's fancy mixed cassimere gold caps, neat grey and brown mixtures, nicely lined and well made up," or "imported linen crash, natural linen color, with six piece top, nicely made," or

7. A Chap and His Cap

IN the larger cities there are custom tailors who can make to your order clothes as good as MICHAELS-STERN and who will charge you from $50.00 to $80.00.

WITHIN easy reach of every community in this country, may be found a reputable clothier who can supply you with MICHAELS-STERN CLOTHES at from $15.00 to $30.00.

DECIDE in favor of MICHAELS-STERN CLOTHES and you also decide in favor of economy of time and money, and of sure, demonstrated-in-advance results.

See the Result of the Camera Man's Investigation
YOUR name on a postal mailed today fetches you a copy of the MICHAELS-STERN Portfolio of *Fashion Photogravures*—eyewitness evidence of *well made, well fitting, reasonably priced* smart clothes.
MICHAELS, STERN & CO., *Largest Manufacturers of Rochester-Made Clothing* ROCHESTER, N.Y.

The group of men at left wear caps, boaters, and fedoras as informal headwear.

the "Harvard golf cap in rich brown mixtures, along with "boy's fancy golden brown mixed or drab fine ribbed corduroy golf cap, nicely made up and lined or a navy blue broadcloth, similar to the golf style, but fuller in the crown, and does not hook down in front, lined with satin."[4] These young chaps followed their elders' example and wore their cloth caps.

Sports are most often associated with the cloth cap. Cricketers early on decided to discard their tall hats in favor of the cap. Advertised and labeled as a golf cap in catalogues, pictured with golfers wearing knickerbockers, sweater vests, or sack coats in fashion illustrations, the casual, fabric cap was a favorite on the

These young gentlemen, obviously members of the same club, all wear the same style and size cap. Their dress and the formal studio setting suggest they belong to a university club.

The cap was a comfortable, casual finishing touch to this gentleman's sack suit.

7. A Chap and His Cap

This gentleman could be foreman of a crew.

fairways. It is still worn by those golfers who have not updated their look to the baseball cap or no hat at all. Vacationers and retirees, often found on the links, wear woven caps of straw or straw substitutes.

The cap was as convenient for work as it was for play. Although it was a suitable head covering, eventually the cloth cap became the badge of the working man, men who became die-hard trade unionists and spawned the idiom "a cloth cap mentality."[5]

The fur cap was worn solely for warmth. It is included in this chapter because of the similarity in shape to the cloth cap. Fur caps could be flat on the top and folded up on all four sides, or be identical to cloth caps, only made of fur.

Whatever the fabric, the cap has been one of the most serviceable head coverings a man could want. Today women have adopted the cap, along with just about every other male fashion item. (I happen to own one in red wool felt.)

8

The Trouble with Hats

"He is known among other things by his hat, but he is an altogether agreeable fellow."
—*Vanity Fair,* March 11, 1893

Idiosyncrasies abound in historical clothing research, especially in the categorization and dating of fashionable civilian men's hats.[1] Institutions that house hats have found them to be difficult to date and categorize because few reference works are devoted to the subject and even fewer actual dates appear on the objects themselves. Hat maker John McMicking says that in all the hats he has seen (and he looks under the interior sweatbands), only two have been dated.

Part of the problem is that men's hats are not as "colorful" as women's hats or scarves or gloves or shoes. To get a grasp on men's hats, one must inspect a vast variety of them, come to understand the manufacturing processes, and cross-reference hundreds of historic photographs and fashion plates. Not many clothing curators or collectors have the time, let alone the inclination, to check all the sources. Written material is scarce, including support for dating and hat identification. One curator did a microscopic fabric and hair analysis but then had nothing with which to compare it, so she ended up using a book of period paintings as a means of general identification.

Men's hats are often stored in obscure locations, on the highest, most unavailable shelves. One collection took two years to uncover. Luckily, it was possible to separate the hats that were suffering from problems of mold and mildew, and send them for repair. One curator wanted to throw away the museum's collection.

Opposite: This young man holds a soft felt hat that has been battered and randomly dented.

For these and other reasons, some of the men's hats on display are either incorrectly labeled or not labeled at all because of lack of information. The hat manufacturing businesses are closing or consolidating, or are too busy to support research into their history and display of their past wares. This is the trouble with hats—no single repository of either manufacturing or styling history exists. One can only pursue a course of complex tracking and cross-referencing, through a maze that even the "Mad Hatter" would have found infuriating.

The obscurity of the collections and the scarcity of written material forced me to follow the trail I intend to describe. It is based on "intelligent gossip" and the few surviving printed documents from the hat manufacturers themselves. Every group interested in the man's hat—manufacturers, retailers, trend setters—has its own "who's who"; from them I gathered every scrap they were willing to share. It is mainly from these men, some third- and fourth-generation hatters, that I learned the history of the men's hatting industry in the United States, Canada, and Great Britain.

The most obvious starting place was with the best-known name brand: Stetson, formerly of Philadelphia, Pennsylvania. Luckily, a western-wear shop owner in Miamisburg, Ohio, when told of my project, insisted that *the* man to interview was John Secrest.[2] He contacted the Stetson Company, got Secrest's number, and I was on my way. I had no idea at that time how difficult this would have been without his help, for Secrest had earlier refused all interviews. His close connection with the John B. Stetson Company, from 1939 to his retirement in 1983, made him a knowledgeable link to this famous company. In our interview he outlined the Stetson manufacturing process, the shaping of a western hat, and the fun he had working with Hollywood stars John Wayne and William Holden, shaping their film-character hats. Along with his oral history, he shared newspaper articles describing both himself and the Stetson Company—articles, I might add, that were rare and are getting rarer as time goes on. eBay has been of great help in getting some of this material, but costs have skyrocketed on all Stetson memorabilia, and for an independent researcher, affordability is key.

So you can imagine that in my first interview, I felt as though I had struck gold. My assumption was that if a retired salesman has so much memorabilia, the company must have its whole history safely stored away at its headquarters (now in New York City). No such luck.

What I didn't realize was the monumental shrinkage in the hat industry, the buy-outs and mergers that had taken place in only the past thirty years. What the remaining hat manufacturers did have to offer were invaluable oral histories from once family-owned businesses like Langenberg (Washington, Missouri), Bollman (Adamstown, Pennsylvania), Biltmore (Guelph, Ontario), Stetson-Resistol (Garland, Texas), and Doran Bros. (Danbury, Connecticut). Although none had many support documents, all had their stories; many of these are included in this book. Each company has changed management and organizational style too frequently for a continuous maintenance of historical data. Thus it is from the bits and pieces that the history of the hatting industry is puzzled together.

The British manufacturing companies also consolidated for a time into one manufacturing corporation, Christy Inc. (The name Allied British Hat Manufacturers was not conducive to sales.) Christy Inc. closed its doors in 2000.[3] Luckily, I got a tour of the factory before it closed. It was like a jolt back one hundred and fifty years, especially watching a worker hand-block a fur felt top hat. The company had few accessible archives; the ones they did retain had been given to the Stockport Heritage Center, where I saw them. Of these catalogues, only seven remain since 1820—three single sheets: 1820, 1842 and 1846; and three multiple-page catalogues, each illustrating approximately two hundred hats for the years 1988, 1911, and 1916.

The search was on. I assumed that Stetson collectors, museum libraries, store catalogues selling all manner of hats would be the obvious sources for dating hats. This was only partly true.

I guessed that perhaps the smaller hat retailers, some of whom had been in business since the late 1800s, might have some of this history—surely a few catalogues in their dusty cellars? Two of the oldest hatters east of the Mississippi are Henry the Hatter, of Detroit (since 1893), and Meyer the Hatter, of New Orleans (since 1894). Both Paul Wassermann, owner of Henry the Hatter, and the Meyer brothers had stories of the retail hatting business from their lifetime experiences, but no memorabilia. What one is able to learn from the remaining smaller hatters spread across the country is a varying degree of understanding of their retail hatting business. The shop owners and their assistants know how to judge excellent hats and are up to date on the newest styles, but don't have much time for the history beyond their immediate family experience, nor were they much interested in dating hats. And why should they be?

It was back to the hats themselves for information. I examined (and continue to examine) approximately two thousand hats. The most obvious identifier, besides the hat shape and material content, is the interior labeling on the hatband and lining, but this is not always conclusive. The imprinted leather sweatbands, if marked, were often worn and then replaced, as one can see in hats in museum collections. The replacement sweatband would be marked with the replacement hatter's mark, not the original manufacturer's—like Lee making hats for J. C. Penney with a Penney's label. Whatever brand hat—Knox, Stetson, Biltmore—it often also carried the name of the retailer on the tip lining or sweatband.[4] Lining markings most often indicated the manufacturer, but these could be replaced, and many earlier hats were unlined. To add to the confusion, many of the hats were finished by the hundreds of hatters that thrived in every town in the country. These small hatters could buy unstyled fur or wool felt hat bodies and then steam them on blocks to their own customers' desired crease and curl. This procedure was also followed in some small

Lining markings most often indicate manufacturers.

retail shops, where hatters were trained to clean and style the hat, not just sell what came already steam-shaped from the larger manufacturers. All of these variations—hats finished and styled from the "body" manufacturers, hats cleaned and relined with the cleaner's label, hats worn so that the lining and sweatband are missing or replaced with no label, and factory hats stripped of their manufacturer's label, then labeled with the retailer's name—impede the identification process.

Looking at trademarks for dating doesn't necessarily help, because they have such a long life span. Madeleine Ginsburg was able to date the Stockport Heritage Museum collection through trademarks, but in some companies, such as Stetson, the same mark can be repeated for years, or even revived. For example, the two Stetson trademarks shown here were registered in 1866

STETSON

and used well into the 1920s.

Another dating possibility would appear to be through the wooden hat block, which hatters use to shape the felt or straw. Roger Hulme, former plant manager for Christy Head Wear, told me he has hundreds of old blocks lying around the factory.[5] So does Gary Rosenthal, product development manager at Hatco and formerly of Stevens Hat Company. He was even able to find a specific 1940s block to use for manufacturing hats for the current swing craze.[6] Each block represents one size of one style of hat. If two hundred styles of hats were manufactured in a fashion season, each style would need a series of blocks ranging in sizes. If these blocks had been dated, or stored in any chronological manner, they would indicate the styles for that year. Unfortunately, most are not. Some old blocks were even taken home and used for firewood.

One should not give up hope, however, because a variety of pictorial evidence can help to identify hat styles and materials. Sales catalogues, although limited, illustrate styles and materials. These catalogues clearly distinguish between name brands and unnamed or generic head wear. Hamley & Co.'s 1942 Cowboy Clothing and Gear Catalogue states, "Same hat, not a Stetson."[7] Montgomery Ward Company, from its inception in 1876, has listed no brand name for any of their men's hats, giving only a hat name ("The Clyde," "The Sheridan"), its weight in ounces, color, and size range; on the other hand, Sears, Roebuck & Company advertised their Stetson by calling it "The World famous J. B. Stetson Sombrero Hat, worn by the most famous scout and guide in the world," accompanied by a line drawing of Buffalo Bill Cody, which relates the hat to Buffalo Bill's period of fame at the turn of the twentieth century.

Above and at left are shown an assortment of hat blocks used for shaping different styles of hats.

8 Smaller suppliers, such as Stockman's Supplies of Denver, Dave Jones of Cody, Wyoming, and Hamley's of Pendleton, Oregon, boldly advertised the Stetson product.[9] What they show parallels what Stetson shows in its catalogues, so if you have a hat similar to their pictures and their dated catalogue, you have a match and a date.

I had hoped that fashion journals would fill in the gaps, since they began publication much earlier, in the mid-eighteenth century.[10] Two such journals, created by the merchant tailors' associations, appeared for men: *The Sartorial Art Journal,* published in the United States, and the *The Sartor,* published in England. Each issue commented on what was appropriate for the well-dressed gentleman and specified style changes for their tailors, including a fully detailed picture and pattern of the latest suit style, complete with fitting and altering instructions. But problems arise in their representation of headwear. In all cases the men are shown wearing the appropriate hat, but when you compare several years of top hats or bowlers, you realize that they are all drawn in a similar manner. One is able to discern only the general type or style of hat appropriate for the specific ensemble. Within each hat category, there is minimal variation in styling. One guesses that this must be an artistic convention, since the Christy catalogue of 1911 included over two hundred styles of hats. In a history of Danbury hatting, W. H. Francis states that in 1822, "hats are dyed in all colors, Black, Brown, Tan, Drab, and in fact almost every shade conceivable."[11] Such variety is absent from the men's fashion journals. These journal collections are also scanty; very few consecutive years remain intact at the New York Public Library or the British Library.[12]

Other publications are more helpful. One is *Vanity Fair*, which pictures men in slightly exaggerated postures (see next page). In ten caricatures that were published between July 1874 and October 1879, ten very different styles of top hats appear. The hats vary in size, color, and manner of wearing. Other sources, such as *The Illustrated London Gazette* and *Frank Leslie's Illustrated Magazine,* go beyond the sartorially stylish to picture men of all classes wearing hats. Since their purpose is to illustrate the news, the clothing depicted is more useful as a cross-reference with the other sources, especially regarding the vast variety of head coverings and how they were individually adapted.

What about photographs? Here people are wearing actual clothing. Very few are dated, but at least you could date the clothing, therefore dating the hat. However, men's hats, once again, provoke a peculiar uncertainty. Men's hats were worn for a much longer

HAT TALK

8. The Trouble with Hats

Opposite: drawing from Vanity Fair; Above: Frank Leslie's Illustrated Newspaper, June 1869.

period than women's rapidly changing fashion statements. Men's hats were passed on or thrown away. Men's hats became items of personal identity and might not be changed when a new suit was purchased. Certainly it appears that general style changes were adopted, but not necessarily annually. The most significant value of photographs, tintypes, and daguerreotypes is in demonstrating how hats can be personalized by individuals shaping and tilting them.

Artists' interpretations are minimally useful. Significant is the artist's depiction of fabric, its distinctive texture and sheen. The artist's purpose is not clothing history, although many items of clothing, including hats, have been found in artist's studios.[13] Different versions of the same style hat appear, especially if a style is made popular in paintings or film. The round low-crowned hats worn by the cowboys in the Remington drawing (facing page) can actually be seen in photographs of cowboys. I have found this hat in museum collections, and I have a 1920s version in my collection. A 1940s reproduction is in another museum, and 1990s reproductions are mass-produced for reenactments and the continually popular Western films. The shape is basically the same, and they are all made from some mixture of fur or wool felt. John B. Stetson marketed his version as the "Boss of the Plains"; the same name is given to current Stetson reproductions. The "Tom Mix" style has a similar long history. So how does one know the difference?

In this case, the name of the hat—Boss of the Plains—makes dating difficult. In another case, identification can be confused by calling a hat a "beaver." Originally a hat made from beaver was of higher quality; consequently, it was the most expensive, because of its finer finish and durability. In the predominantly wool-felt manufacturing town of Reading, Pennsylvania, manufacturers called their hats "Ram Beavers," alluding to the use of wool instead of fur.[14] Most museums and antique dealers (often on eBay) refer to any top hat as a beaver hat, when these hats actually are made from a silk plush substitute or mixtures of other animal furs.

Louis Holberg (right) and friend.

In fact, very few fur felt hats are found in collections, perhaps two out of one hundred in the major collections. Calling all top hats "beavers" leaves collectors and curators perplexed and misinformed.

What, then, determines the age of a hat? One must look first at the substance and shape. For example, is it wool or fur felt, silk, Ecuadorian straw, paper straw, Luten straw? Does it have a cardboard lining, a plastic or leather sweatband, a manufacturer's label? Does it have a narrow or broad brim, a high or shallow crown, hand or machine creasing?

The physical condition of the hat can give many clues. A two-hundred-year-old hat will differ in fiber content from a reproduction. One specialist realized this when cataloging the Stockport Heritage hats. Their fresh silk shine was the first indication that they were not from the 1840s. Trademark identification verified this conclusion, revealing that they were a set of reproduction silk top hats made in the 1920s.[15] Generally, in older felt hats, the felt is thinner. Originally, all hats were sold with an "open crown," indicating no factory creasing; they were meant to be creased by the retailer or, more often, by the wearer. A quality felt was so soft and pliable that the crease could be blown into it.[16] Hats made from wool lack the durability of fur felt hats, and they feel rougher to the touch. A high percentage of beaver fur causes the hat to feel extremely smooth to the touch whatever the final surface hair length.[17] The more beaver fur, the smoother to the touch, and the more durable.[18]

Hats have changed. But hats have achieved much more than change. Their meaning has changed, and it is the meaning of clothing that has become the most fascinating topic of study. Dating, beyond general trends, is possibly the least interesting aspect of the hat. Study the hats, place the shape into a general historical time period, check for any identifying labels, feel and look at their material. But consider also who wore them, and in what sartorial combinations, for it is how each hat takes on the personality of its wearer, how it functions within the sartorial combination of class, occupation, and style that gives depth to a small but significant portion of hat history.

Appendix

A Tribute to Jeff Fried and the National Hat Museum

Jeffrey W. Fried's dream was to create a museum devoted to hats. In 1998 this dream came true in the form of the National Hat Museum, the first in the United States to have hats as its only focus.

Jeff Fried started collecting hats when he was five-years-old and continued this search throughout the rest of his life. Jeff amassed an extraordinary collection—helmets, hat accessories, and hat-making tools from nearly two dozen countries. His goal in life was to display them, talk about them, and educate whoever would listen to the stories about his hats

Each piece of his collection contains a story—about who we are, where we came from, and where we may be headed. And each piece has its own history, from who made it to who wore it. History is not only about dates, names, places, wars, and boundaries; the individual stories of people contain the truth of history, too.

To that end Jeff wanted the museum to document each artifact as fully as possible.

The museum did not have its own permanent display facilities, but some of the collection could always be seen at the Mad Hatter's Bake Shop in Durham, North Carolina. There Jeff displayed a changing array of hats. One display included coal miners' helmets, two centuries of fire helmets from four countries, police hats from all over the world, hats and head dresses from the Old West, a Red Cross display, and two cases of women's high-fashion hats.

Jeff died in December 2001. He got as far as incorporating the museum and setting up a Web site which can be visited at hatmuseum@yahoo.com. After meeting with Jeff at the Mad Hatter's Bake Shop a number of times, going to his home where every square inch of space held a hat, and listening to him tell stories of the people who wore this hat and that hat, I feel enriched by his love of his collection and the scholarship he devoted to his subject—hats of all kinds, makes, and uses. Whenever you look at a hat or add one to your collection, remember Jeff Fried who collected the lives and stories of more than 3000 hats and couldn't wait to get to that next flea market to see what he would discover next. Think of him and tip your hat.

John Wm. McMicking: Historic Hat Maker *Extraordinaire*!

Each year on October 23, John McMicking sends out St. Clement's Day cards. St. Clement is the patron saint of hatters. John loves hats and has loved and collected them since he was six years old. On the walls of his family's hundred-year-old home in Dundas, Ontario, drawings and paintings picture John dressed in period clothing always wearing—what else?—the appropriate hat. John not only wears hats, but he also makes and sells them.

He has supplied the Lincoln Museum in Fort Wayne, Indiana, with a replica of Abraham Lincoln's top hat. He makes all manner of hats for the Stratford Theatre Festival, the Shaw Festival, and the Canadian Opera Company. When museums or re-enactors need a certain style, he can make it. "I can make anything that can be described, if I can get the proper materials."

His expertise includes the history of hatting as well. "Most hats evolved slowly, through use, from an earlier style, and the practical, over time, often turned into the whimsical. The tri-corner hat started out as a plain, low-crown, wide brim hat. But with the brim folded up, it becomes the familiar patriot's symbol."

For information, and definitely a hat, call: 905-627-7472

The Beaver (Castor Fiver)

The North American continent was explored and trading established in the quest for profitable animal pelts. Since beaver made the finest, tightest felt, beaver was most sought after in the colder, northern parts of the United States and Canada. Near extinction of the beaver by the early 1900s forced the replacement of beaver felt hats, by then the most expensive, with man-made French silk plush.

Beaver fur is the most desirable, and today rare, fur used in making a fur felt hat. The finest of the beaver furs comes from the soft gray underbelly of this semi-aquatic animal, which is why the better hats made with this fur are referred to as "silver-belly." The fur of beavers and other hat-fur-bearing animals that live in the wild provide better fur than animals raised in captivity, due to the resiliency and "water-proofing" qualities obtained in nature. Winter fur is considered best since it is thicker and finer; summer coats tend to be thinner and therefore provide inferior fur.

To obtain the underfur, all the coarse guard-hairs are separated, either by hand-bow plucking or by cleaning machines. When the hairs are blown through the many-chambered cleaning machines, the coarser, heavier hairs and other detritus fall to the bottom, allowing the much lighter and finer furs to continue through to the end of the machine and on to the next stage in the felting process, which is making the hat cone.

Hat makers say that a 100 percent beaver fur hat is a bit too soft to shape. They prefer to mix in a small percentage of hare, nutria, or other fur, enabling the felt to be more structurally stout and better able to hold the shape of the hat. It is generally acknowledged that beaver fur makes the strongest felt because it "felts" (pulls, knots, and interweaves), "locking" together more tightly and permanently than other furs. This is due partly to the microscopic scales on the individual fur fibers.

The Nutria (Myocastor Coypus)

The finest Hats in the World are Made in America, and the Finest American Hats are Made from Clear Nutria Fur. Nutria Fur comes from a small South American animal, greatly resembling the beaver, but much more plentiful. The skins of these animals are imported into this country in immense quantities by manufacturers of **Fine Hats**. The fur is thoroughly cleaned, combed and pounced, being finally transformed into felt, out of which the finest hats are made. Nutria fur is particularly desirable for this purpose as it is very fine soft and silky, and when prepared into felt contains no lumps, impurities or other objectionable matter. A clear Nutria fur hat is as soft and smooth as a piece of silk, will retain its shape and color and will outwear any other kind of hat made.

—Sears, Roebuck & Company, 1897

When you read the label inside a fedora or western hat—mainly from the 1900s to the 1950s—you may sometimes see the statement "Made of the finest Nutria fur." The nutria is native to Brazil, Bolivia, Paraguay, Uruguay, Argentina, and Chile. Today nutria live in the south-central United States, especially in the marshes of Louisiana. Nutria are semi-aquatic, inhabiting marshes, lake edges, and sluggish streams, much like the beaver whose fur is so desirable for hat making. They are strictly vegetarian, living on roots in and along the waterways. They are in general yellowish or reddish brown with guard hairs that conceal the soft, thick, velvety dark gray underfur, which is the part used in felting. Nutria fur is the only other fur considered to be on a par with beaver, which is why it is mentioned specifically in catalogues, advertisements, and labels, whereas other fur fibers, such as hare, muskrat, and rabbit, are not.

APPENDIX

The Museum of Hatting - Stockport

Come and see the UK's only museum dedicated to the hatting industry!

- Working Machinery
- William White's Shop
- William Plant's Hat Block Workshop
- Audio Visual Room
- Mad Hatter's Tea Room

OPEN EVERY SUNDAY

Stockport Metropolitan Borough Council

Rare Hat Catalogues

In the early twentieth century, hat catalogues were supplied to every hat dealer across the country and across the world. Today few remain. This is why the following pages are devoted to excerpts from Stetson catalogues for 1913, 1914, and 1922. They also serve as a reminder of the numerous variations available in each hat style.

The catalogues were produced as single, unbound 9 x 12-inch pages enclosed in a folder.

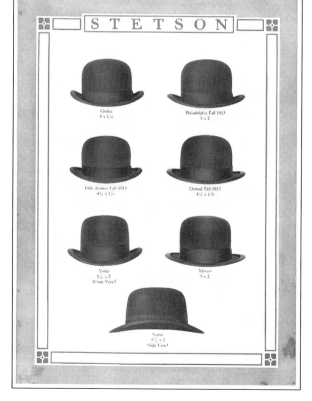

APPENDIX

APPENDIX

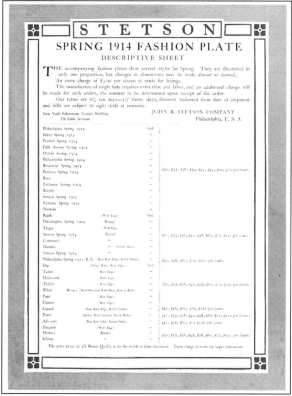

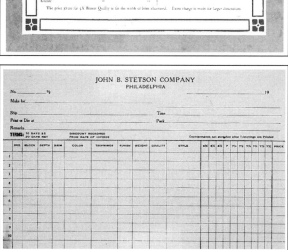

APPENDIX

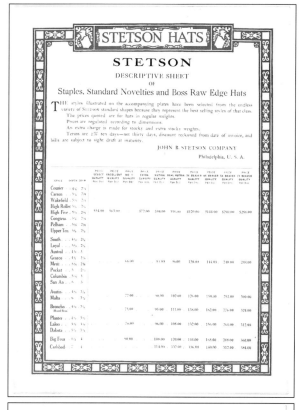

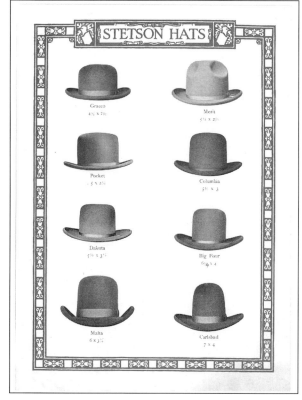

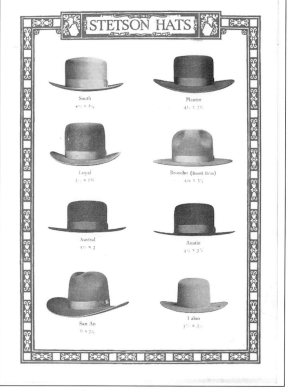

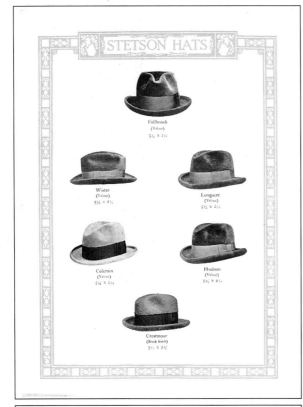
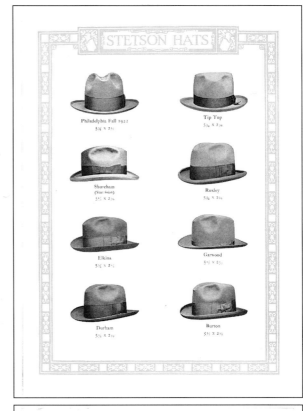
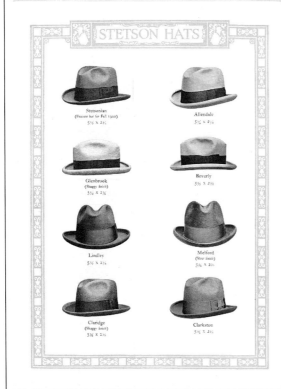

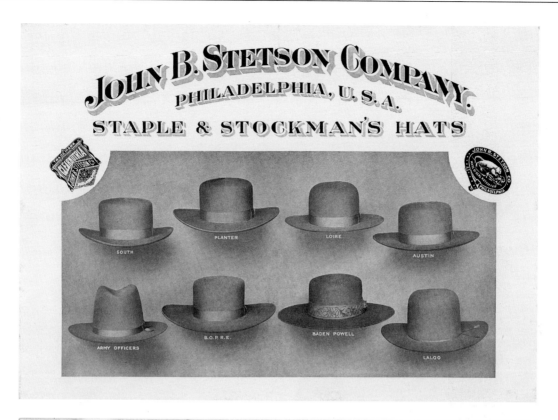

Graham Thompson in his hat shop, Optima, in Chicago.

Notes

1. Danbury, Connecticut

1. William Devlin, *We Crown Them All: An Illustrated History of Danbury*, (Woodland Hills, CA: Windsor Publications, Inc., 1984), 47.
2. Ibid., 52.
3. Ibid., 48.
4. Debbie Henderson, "The Forming Machine: How the Manufacturing of Hats Went from 6 to 600 per Day," *Chronicle of the Early American Industries Association* (Vol. 51, No. 3, September, 1998), 75–79. The forming machine is so crucial because it is the first step in the making or forming of a hat body. Loose, cleaned fur is blown onto a perforated, revolving metal cone. Once there is an even layer of fur, the whole cone is dipped in hot water, then carefully slipped off the cone. Robert Doran estimates that each forming machine can produce 10,000 dozen hat bodies a year. In 1900 in the United States there were 350 to 400 forming machines; in Europe there were 900 formers. In 1946 in the United States there were 200 and in Europe approximately 400. In 1996 there were about 20 in the United States and possibly 30 in western Europe.
5. Robert Doran, interviews by author, Danbury, Connecticut, 10 October 1996 and 22 May 1997. The term "finishing machine" refers to those specific machines that "finish" a hat. They include pouncing machines that sand the surface of a felt hat to the desired smoothness or shine, routing machines that trim the brim edge to a uniform width, and a series of steaming and ironing machines that shape the crowns, curl or flange the brims, and give the hat its final flair. The tip lining, sweatband, optional brim band, and hat band are individually hand-sewn onto the hat in a separate department. The only machines used in this final process are industrial sewing machines, which are considered separate from the hat finishing machines.
6. Edward Mott Woolley, *A Century of Hats and The Hats of the Century*, (Danbury, CT: The Mallory Hat Company, Inc., 1923), 21.
7. John Reed Crawford, interview by author, London, England, 17 July 1997.
8. John Secrest, interview by author, Tucson, Arizona, 23 March 1994. This interview can be found in *Cowboys and Hatters: Bond Street, Sagebrush and the Silver Screen* by the author (Yellow Springs, OH: Wild Goose Press, 1996), 33–41. John Milano, interview by author, Garland, Texas, 8 January 1996. Robert Doran, interview. Cultural myth blames John F. Kennedy for the demise of the man's hat because he did not wear the traditional silk top hat at his inauguration (even though he was fitted for one). The more realistic view held by

hat manufacturers is that the decline was a slower evolution, starting after the boom in hat wearing from 1900 to the 1920s and ending with a crash in the 1970s. They cite the automobile and the resultant change in lifestyle as the prime catalyst.

Once the felt hat evolved from handmade to machine made, the production process was divided into two areas (often two buildings or locations)—the "back shop" and the "front shop." The back shop takes the raw fur (hare, beaver, nutria, etc.), cleans it, blows it over a form that shapes it into a large cone, then massages the cone in scalding hot water, causing it to shrink to one third its original size. It is then stretched into a rough hat shape (it looks like a broad-brimmed western hat with a round crown that has been left out in the rain for weeks). These fur forms, now called raw "hat bodies," are then dried and shaved of their randomly protruding long hairs. Stacks of raw bodies can be sent to the finishing floors in the home factory or shipped to other finishing factories or small hat makers. When the industry began to downsize in the 1970s, back shops often supplied numerous front shops across the country.

2. Gentlemen's Hatters and Their Hats

1. Much of this basic information on Knox and Dunlap comes from a booklet produced by the Knox Company in 1929, *The Story of Two Famous Hatters* by Robert R. Updegraff (New York: Knox Hat Company, 1926). The John B. Stetson Company had similar pamphlets, as did Mallory and Lee. One might assume that the writers glamorized their founders' lives and achievements, but in cross-checking this information with other references, I have found the summations, on the whole, to be accurate.
2. Ibid., 10.
3. This is a typical set-up for a hatter working in a city. James Locke and Co. Ltd. of London has occupied #6 St. James's Street (and the neighboring building) since 1676. You may visit there today and see the retail shop on the ground floor. Currently, one of the upper floors is used to house and sell their women's lines.
4. Updegraff, 22.
5. This is the constant complaint from hatters about those corporations that buy out the older hatting companies: "The management doesn't know anything about hatting!" This trend is indicative of a change from the production of a craft item to a mass-produced item.
6. Updegraff, 19–20.
7. Ibid., 26.
8. Ibid., 10.

9. The John B. Stetson Company has used the association between their hats and famous personalities to the maximum during the twentieth century. Their 1929 hat catalogue pictures hats on famous movie stars only. Stetson was so persistent with this campaign that the western hat is now called a Stetson, even though other companies—Resistol, Beaver Brand Hats, Biltmore Hats, and Justin, the Milano Hat Co.—made and continue to make western style hats.
10. Updegraff, 22.
11. Ibid., 37.
12. Ibid., 43.
13. Ibid., 55.
14. Ibid., 70.
15. Richard Albert, interview by author, 14 December 1995. Dick Albert has been with the Resistol Company as a sales representative since 1947. He is also married to Harry Rolnick's niece. Dick has spent his whole life in the hat business. His complete interview appears in *Cowboys and Hatters: Bond Street, Sagebrush and the Silver Screen*, by the author (Yellow Springs, OH, 1996), 42–46.
16. Ibid., 43–45.
17. Jan Lewis, interview by author, 17 July 2001.
18. Roy Langenberg, interview by author, 8 January 1996.
19. Many of the men interviewed—among them Bob Doran and George Rafferty—talk about the number of formers. A more complete description of the forming machine can be found in an article by the auther, "The Forming Machine," *Chronicle of the Early American Industries Association* (Vol. 51, No. 3, September, 1998),75–79.
20. "The Bollman Companies: The First Two Generations," *The Bollman cHatter* (1st Quarter, 1987), 4.
21. "The Bollman Companies: The Third Generation," *The Bolman cHatter* (3rd Quarter, 1987), 5.
22. Ibid.
23. *Eversince: Evoluzione e Stile* Brochure (Alessandria: Borsalino Company, 2000), 11.
24. Fortunately, many of those hats may be seen pictured in the book *Men's Hats* by Adele Campione (Milan: BE-MA, Editrice, 1988).
25. Borsalino Company flyer (Alessandria: Borsalino Company, 2000), 1.
26. Ibid.
27. Ibid., 2. Claudio Mennuni, interview by author, Alessandria, Italy, 18 May 1999.
28. Since I was unable to visit their factory, I have no further information. Their Web site is www.tonakhats.cz
29. To see pictures of all the machines Bob Doran mentioned in his interview, check the December 1999 issue of *Chronicle of the Early American Industries Association* for the article "The Making of a Felt Hat," by the author.

3. The System of Hat Making

1. J. Leander Bishop, *A History of American Manufacturers*, vol. II (1868; reprint, New York: Augustus M. Kelly, Publishers, 1966), 509.

4. Everyman and His Bowler

1. Fred Miller Robinson, *The Man in the Bowler Hat: Its History and Iconography* (London: The University of North Carolina Press, 1993), 46. Mr. Robinson goes into great detail, using artists (Magritte), writers (Beckett, Kundera), and actors (Chaplin, Laurel and Hardy) to explore and explain how such a simple clothing item, the bowler, can accumulate multiple layers of cultural innuendo, especially for the middle class. "The bowler hat is a sign of modern times—that is to say, the times of the emerging and expanding modern middle classes" (4). "The blur of stereotypical headgear represented a blurring of class boundaries" (59).
2. Diana deMarly, *Working Dress: A History of Occupational Clothing* (New York: Holmes and Meier Publishers, Inc., 1987), 149.
3. As quoted in Robinson, 89.
4. *Montgomery Ward Catalogues* 1876–1950 (Chicago: Montgomery Ward & Co., 1900), 948. Luckily for researchers, the University of Wyoming's American Heritage Center in Laramie, Wyoming, has a complete set of *Montgomery Ward Catalogues*.
5. John McMicking, interview by author, Dundas, Ontario, 31 October 2001. Christy Hat Wear Company (now Patey Ltd. of London) was the maker of many of Lock's hats (bowlers and top hats especially), but the hats were made and finished by Christy's. Lock's at #6 have long since become more sellers of hats and not makers (with the exception of their new line of women's millinery). Lock's had a business association with Christy for years and one of the family served on the board of directors. Christy's provided finished hats to Lock & Co. with the Lock & Co. label. The same hats were for sale elsewhere with the Christy's of London label, Harrod's label, G.A. Dunn & Co. label, etc.
6. *Christy & Co. Catalogues* 1899, 1911 and 1916 (Stockport: The Christy Hat Co., 1899, 1911, 1916), pp. 2–3, 3–4, 2–3 respectively. For those interested, the sizes of bowlers ranged in 1899 from a crown of $4\frac{7}{8}$ and brim of $1\frac{7}{8}$ to a crown of $5\frac{7}{8}$ and brim of $2\frac{1}{2}$; in 1911 a crown of $4\frac{5}{8}$ (boys 4) and brim of $1\frac{5}{8}$ (boys $1\frac{5}{8}$) to a crown of $5\frac{1}{4}$ and a brim of $2\frac{1}{8}$; in 1916 a crown of $4\frac{7}{8}$ and a brim of 2 to a crown of $5\frac{1}{8}$ and a brim of $2\frac{1}{8}$. Not only has the variety in sizes diminished but also the variety in styles.
7. *Montgomery Ward Catalogue*, 1920, 265. The "Open-Road" style hat has a moderately wide brim, flanged up on the sides; down the top center of the crown runs a crease front to back; on either side of the top crease is a parallel indentation that runs midway down the crown. It was a popular western style worn all during the twentieth century and became LBJ's signature hat.
8. *Chas. P. Shipley Saddlery and Mercantile Co. Catalog No. 28* (Kansas City: Chas. P. Shipley), 59.
9. *Stockman's Supplies* (Denver: The Denver Dry Goods Company, 1941), 7.
10. Frank Whitbourn, *Mr. Lock of St. James's Street* (London: Heineman, 1971), 120. The chapter pertaining to the bowler is pp. 121–127.
11. John McMicking, interview by author, Dundas, Ontario, 7 June 2001.
12. Whitbourn, 120.
13. Ibid., 123.
14. A conformateur is a hand-operated mechanical device that is placed onto the head so that the moveable calipers can conform to the unique shape of each individual's head, which shape is then transferred to a second device, and recorded on a small card for future sizing. The hat shop then has a permanent record of their customer's head size and shape from which future orders can be shaped.
15. Whitbourn, 120.
16. McMicking interview and Whitbourn, 121.
17. *Montgomery Ward & Co.'s Catalogue*, No. 66, 1900, 948.
18. This phrase is used by John Wayne in the film *The Fighting Kentuckian* (Hollywood: Republic Pictures, 1949). While visiting Lock's in London, I overheard a conversation between the hatter and his customer in which the customer was getting his gray felt top hat stretched to fit his head. It had been willed to him by his father-in-law. At $400 for a new one, there is reason to continue the practice.
19. Walter Rhodes, interview by author, Yellow Springs, Ohio, 24 June 2001. Not only is the bowler king, but it apparently still has significance to the world of finance. Molly Baker has a bowler pictured on the cover of her new book, *High-Flying: Adventures in the Stock Market*.

5. How the Fedora Got Its "Snap"

1. Bishop, *A History of American Manufacturers,* vol. III, 499.
2. David Bensman, *The Practice of Solidarity: American Hat*

Finishers in the Nineteenth Century (Chicago: University of Illinois Press, 1985), 132.

3. *Sears, Roebuck & Company Catalogue* (Chicago: Sears, Roebuck & Co., Inc., 1897), 232–233.

4. My husband wears an Icaro crusher he bought at the Borsalino Hat Company in Italy. It can easily be rolled into a tube for traveling and then reshaped by hand. The Borsalino salesman demonstrated all its advantages during our visit and interview, 17 June 1999. Adele Campione's booklet *Men's Hats* (Milano: BE-MA Editrice, 1988) contains photographs of hats from the Borsalino hat collection housed in the Alessandria Museum. The hats are beautifully photographed and tell a story of their own, but the supporting written material contains many incorrect descriptions, which may be the result of a loose translation from the accompanying Italian.

5. Updegraff, *The Story of Two Famous Hatters*, 70.

6. The Disposable Straw

1. Bishop, *A History of American Manufacturers,* vol. II, 78. As some might think this story social legend, it is doubly supported by a corresponding account by Peter Boileau, and a letter from the then Mrs. Baker (Betsy Metcalf) in 1858. For a very complete explanation of the straw hat industry, tools, and history in Great Britain, see Charles Freeman, *Luton and the Hat Industry* (Luton: The Borough of Luton Museum and Art Gallery, 1953).

2. James Laver, *Costume and Fashion: A Concise History* (London: Thames and Hudson, 1995), 221.

3. *Taylor Bros. & Co. Catalogue* (Chicago: Taylor Bros. Inc., 1889), 72–89.

4. Straw hats were always popular because of their advantages: inexpensively hand-crafted of local materials. The British Museum has two paintings in which each woven straw hat is identical to modern straw hats; one is a Mexican broad-brimmed sombrero in *The Virgin and Child with Saints* by Pisanello, ca. 1440–55; the other is a western style straw in *St. Margaret* by Zurbaran, ca. 1630–35.

5. *Sears, Roebuck & Co.* (Chicago: Sears, Roebuck & Co. Inc., 1897), 235. *Taylor Bros. & Co.*, 1889.

6. S. Grant Sergot, "The Original Panama Hat," advertising flyer (Bisbee, AZ: Optimo Custom Hatworks, 1996). Martine Buchet, *Panama, a Legendary Hat* (Paris: Editions Assouline, 1995). Tom Miller, *The Panama Hat Trail* (New York: William Morrow and Company, 1986). Today Montecristis start at $400 and can go up to $4000 if made by one of the few remaining craftsmen in Ecuador. It is very difficult to find other weavers to learn this craft with the cities acting as a constant lure from traditional life styles.

7. Buchet, *Panama, A Legendary Hat*, 58. For the lover of the Panama hat, this book is an exquisite pictorial tribute to the history of the hats and to the people who hand-weave their fine product.

8. Ibid., 30.

9. Graham Thompson of Optimo Hat Company in Chicago, Illinois, is one such adventurer. He carries a full stock of current Panama hats and the rare Montecristis, ranging in price from $50 to $2000.

10. Madeleine Ginsburg, *The Hat: Trends and Traditions* (London: Studio Editions, Ltd., 1990), 153.

11. Whitbourn, Mr. Lock of St. James's Street, 126.

12. Helen Hollberg, interview by author, 12 July 2001.

7. A Chap and His Cap

1. *White & Davis Parcel Post Catalogue* No. 23 & No. 34 (Pueblo, CO: White & Davis Company, 1924, 1929), 11, 15.

2. Whitbourn, 126.

3. *Sears, Roebuck & Co. Catalogue* (Chicago: Sears, Roebuck & Co., 1887), no page numbers given. Young ladies are pictured with tam o'shanters, middy caps, and a more gathered version of the cap, simply called a silk cap.

4. Ibid.

5. Whitbourn, 126.

8. The Trouble with Hats

1. Ann Hollander in her book, *Seeing Through Clothes* (New York: Viking Press, 1975), writes extensively on the inability to discover the past, especially its fashionable nuances, because the past was pictorially interpreted by artists who used stylization as part of their pictorial means. It is this interpretation, not accuracy, that is transmitted through time.

2. Debbie Henderson, *Cowboys and Hatters: Bond Street, Sagebrush and the Silver Screen (*Yellow Springs, OH: Wild Goose Press, 1996). This book includes the interview with John Secrest.

3. The Stockport Heritage Museum has a Web site, Stockport.com, which gives all the information about the history and closing of the Christy plant in Stockport.

4. A tip lining is the label at the tip of the crown lining. I have

seen stamps at the various hat manufacturers that produce their own lining, in turn stamping specific logos for their various clients. Sometimes the manufacturer's name is nowhere on the hat, especially for prestigious brands like Burberry, which bought their hats from Christy Head Wear.

5. Roger Hulme, interview by author, Stockport, England, 19 July 1994.

6. Gary Rosenthal, interview by author, Garland, Texas, 30 December 1998.

7. *Cowboy Clothing and Gear: The Complete Hamley Catalogue of 1942* (Pendleton, OR: Hamley & Company, 1942), 151.

8. *Sears, Roebuck Catalogue*, 1906 edition (New York: Crown Publishers, reprint, 1969), 234.

9. *Stockman's Supplies* (Denver: Stockman's Company, 1941), 7.

10. Madeleine Ginsburg, *An Introduction to Fashion Illustration* (London: Studio Editions, 1980).

11. W. H. Francis, *History of the Hatting Trade in Danbury, Conn. from its Commencement in 1780 to the Present Time* (Danbury: H. & L. Osborne Publishers, 1860), 10.

12. *The Sartorial Art Journal* reprint (New York: Jno. J. Mitchell Company, 1891–1910) and *The Sartor* (London: 1870–1872).

13. The Frederic Remington and G. Koerner studios are installed at the Buffalo Bill Historical Center. The Charles Russell studio is set up at the Russell Museum in Great Falls, Montana. All three contain clothing, including hats.

14. Paul E. Werckshagen, "St. Clement's Art in Old Readingtown," *Historical Review of Berks County* (Vol. 1, No. 3, April, 1936), 83–88.

15. Tessa Wiley, interviews by author, Stockport, England, 25 June 1994 and 2 July 1995.

16. John Milano, interview by author, 8 January 1996. John demonstrated "blowing a crease."

17. The fur on the outside of a fur felt hat can be shaved to a smooth suede finish or left long in a velour finish. This is controlled in the manufacturing process, not in the styling.

18. Every hatter I have interviewed (approximately fifty or more) has agreed on the excellence of beaver fur. They feel that hare is a close second, and considerably more available.

Bibliography

Albert, Richard. Interview by author. Dallas, Texas, 18 December 1994.

Bensman, David. *The Practice of Solidarity: American Hat Finishers in the Nineteenth Century*. Chicago: University of Illinois Press, 1985.

Bishop, Leander J. *A History of American Manufacturers From 1608 to 1860*. Reprint, New York: Augustus M. Kelley Publishers, 1966.

"Bollman Companies: The First Two Generations, The." *The Bollman cHatter* (1st Quarter, 1987): 4–5.

"Bollman Companies: The Third Generation, The." *The Bollman cHatter* (3rd Quarter, 1987): 4–5.

Brummell, Beau. *Male and Female Costume*. New York: Benjamin Blom, 1972.

Buchet, Martine. *Panama, a Legendary Hat*. Paris: Editions Assouline, 1995.

Campione, Adele. *Men's Hats*. Milano: BE-MA Editrice, 1988.

Collins, Stephen A. *Two Centuries of Hat Making: Danbury's Famous Tale*. Danbury, Connecticut: Danbury Tricentennial Committee, 1985.

deMarly, Diana. *Working Dress: A History of Occupational Clothing*. New York: Holmes and Meier Publishers, Inc., 1987.

Devlin, William E. *We Crown Them All: An Illustrated History of Danbury*. Woodland Hills, CA: Windsor Publications, Inc., 1984.

Doran, Robert. Interviews by author. Danbury, Connecticut, 19 October 1996 and 22 May 1997.

Eversince: Evoluzione e Stile. Alessandria, Italy: Borsalino Company, 1999.

W. H. Francis, *History of the Hatting Trade in Danbury, Conn. from its Commencement in 1780 to the Present Time*. Danbury, Connecticut: H. & L. Osborne Publishers, 1860.

Charles Freeman, *Luton and the Hat Industry*. Luton: The Borough of Luton Museum and Art Gallery, 1953.

Gilbert, Martin. *Churchill: A Photographic Portrait*. New York: Wing Books, 1974.

Ginsburg, Madeleine. *The Hat: Trends and Traditions*. London: Studio Editions, Ltd., 1990.

———. *An Introduction to Fashion Illustration*. London: Studio Editions, 1980.

Hatter's Gazette, The. London: The Organ of the Hat, Hosiery and Waterproof Trades, December 1900; April and June 1912; July 1915.

Henderson, Debbie. *Cowboys and Hatters: Bond Street, Sagebrsuh, and the Silver Screen*. Yellow Springs, Ohio:

Wild Goose Press, 1996.

———. "The Forming Machine." *Chronicle of the Early American Industries Association* (Vol. 51., No., 3, September, 1998): 75–79.

———. *The Handmade Felt Hat.* Yellow Springs, Ohio: Wild Goose Press, 2001.

———. "The Making of a Felt Hat." *Chronicle of the Early American Industries Association* (Vol. 52, No. 4, December, 1999): 155–160.

———. *The Top Hat: An Illustrated History.* Yellow Springs, OH: Wild Goose Press, 2000.

Hollander, Ann. *Seeing Through Clothes.* New York: Viking Press, 1975.

Hudson, Ben R. "Carnival in the High Andes." *Off the Beaten Track.* New York: United Nations, 1958.

Israel, Fred L., editor. *1897 Sears Roebuck Catalogue.* New York: Chelsea House Publishers, 1976.

Lambert, Jack. Interview by author. New York City, New York, 4 March 1998.

Langenberg, Roy. Interview by author. Washington, Missouri, 8 January 1996.

Laver, James. *Costume and Fashion: A Concise History.* London: Thames and Hudson, 1995.

Lewis, Jan. Interview by author. Conroe, Texas, 17 July 2001.

McMicking, John. Interview by author. Dundas, Ontario, 7 June 2001.

Mennuni, Claudio. Interview by author. Alessandria, Italy, 18 May 1999.

Milano, John. Interview by author. Garland, Texas., 8 January 1996.

Miller, Tom. *The Panama Hat Trail.* New York: William Morrow and Company, 1986.

Montgomery Ward Catalogues, 1877–1950. Chicago: Montgomery Ward & Co., 1877–1950.

Pischke, Richard. Interview by author. Philadelphia, Pennsylvania., 10 March 1999.

Posey, Robert. Interview by author. Dallas, Texas, 30 December 1998.

Reed-Crawford. "A Hat-Maker Remembers: A Conversation with John Reed-Crawford." *Costume Society* (Vol. 32, 1998).

Rhodes, Walter. Interview by author. Yellow Springs, Ohio, 24 June 2001.

Robinson, Fred Miller. *The Man in the Bowler Hat: Its History and Iconography.* London: The University of North Carolina Press, 1993.

Rosenthal, Gary. Interview by author. Garland, Texas., 30 December 1998.

Sears, Roebuck & Co. Catalogue. Chicago: Sears, Roebuck & Co., 1897.

Secrest, John. Interview by author. Tuscon, Arizona., 21 March 1994.

Sergot, S. Grant. "The Original Panama Hat," advertising flyer. Bisbee, Arizona: Optimo Custom Hatworks, 1996.

Taylor Bros. & Co. Hat Catalogue. Chicago: Taylor Bros. & Co., 1889.

Tien, Ellen. "Caps, Caps, Read All About 'Em!." *The New York Times* (Sunday, March 25, 2001).

Updegraff, Robert R. *The Story of Two Famous Hatters.* New York: The Knox Hat Company, 1926.

Werckshagen, Paul E. "St. Clement's Art in Old Readingtown," *Historical Review of Berks County*, Vol. 1, No. 3, April 1936, 83–88.

Whitbourn, Frank. *Mr. Lock of St. James's Street.* London: Heineman, 1971.

White & Davis Parcel Post Catalogue No. 23 and No. 34. Pueblo, Colorado: White and Davis Company, 1924 and 1929.

Woolley, Edward Mott. *A Century of Hats and The Hats of the Century.* Danbury, Connecticut: The Mallory Hat Company, Inc., 1923.

About the Author

Debbie Henderson, Ph.D., is currently the costume designer for the Wittenberg University Theatre Department in Springfield, Ohio. In her work, Dr. Henderson researches clothing worn in other centuries and other countries while attempting to discover the attitudes clothing conveys and inspires. This interest prompted her interdisciplinary doctoral work on the history and manufacture of the man's hat, undertaken through the Union Institute in Cincinnati, Ohio. Her research resulted in the creation of an exhibit about the man's hat that contains over a hundred hats and related visual materials, and which has been shown at museums around the country. She is also a designer of residential and commercial spaces. Dr. Henderson is the author of *Cowboys & Hatters: Bond Street, Sagebrush, & the Silver Screen* (Wild Goose Press, 1996), *The Top Hat: An Illustrated History* (Wild Goose Press, 2000) *The Handmade Felt Hat* (Wild Goose Press, 2001), and numerous journal articles.